MONASTIC WISDOM SERIES: NUMBER SIXTY-NINE

# Blessed Weakness

MONASTIC WISDOM SERIES: NUMBER SIXTY-NINE

# Blessed Weakness

## Homilies for Sundays in Year A

*André Louf, OCSO*

Translated by Paul Rowe, OCSO

Cistercian Publications
cistercianpublications.org

LITURGICAL PRESS
Collegeville, Minnesota
litpress.org

A Cistercian Publications title published by Liturgical Press

**Cistercian Publications**
Editorial Offices
161 Grosvenor Street
Athens, Ohio 45701
cistercianpublications.org

Cover image courtesy of Getty Images.

Translated from André Louf, *Heureuse Faiblesse: Homilies pour les dimanches de l'année*. Paris: Desclée de Brouwer, 1998.

Biblical quotations are translated directly from André Louf's text by Paul Rowe.



**Library of Congress Cataloging-in-Publication Data**

Names: Louf, André author | Rowe, Paul, 1971– translator
Title: Blessed weakness : homilies for Sundays in year A / André Louf, OCSO ; translated by Paul Rowe, OCSO.
Other titles: Heureuse faibless. English
Description: Collegeville, Minnesota : Liturgical Press, [2025] | Series: Monastic wisdom series ; number 69 | Summary: "This volume contains Dom André's homilies on the Gospel passages for year A of the church's three-year liturgical cycle. These homilies reflect Dom André's spiritual insights about the wisdom in the teachings of Christ. The title conveys a favorite theme of Dom André's: God's special love for humans in their weakness, manifested in Jesus' leaving behind his glory to become one of us in weakness, living among and ministering to the poor"— Provided by publisher.
Identifiers: LCCN 2025017558 | ISBN 9780879073077 trade paperback
Subjects: LCSH: Sermons, French—Translations into English | BISAC: RELIGION / Christian Ministry / Preaching | RELIGION / Christianity / Catholic
Classification: LCC BV4254.F7 L6813 2025 | DDC 252/.02—dc23/eng/20250715
LC record available at https://lccn.loc.gov/2025017558

# Contents

# Foreword

The four New Testament gospels, Matthew, Mark, Luke, and John, present Jesus as a teacher and rabbi. As the Son of God incarnate, this rabbi reveals to us both the mysteries of the divinity and a way of life to cultivate our intimacy with God. Abbot André Louf, OCSO, embodies this charism of teaching and through his meditative reflections offers insights into the ways of deepening our relationship with God.

Dom André, as he is referred to in our Cistercian Order, was born in 1929 in Leuven, Belgium. In 1947, he entered the Trappist-Cistercian abbey of Mont-des-Cats, France, making his solemn profession and monastic consecration in 1954. He attended the Pontifical Biblical Institute and the Pontifical Gregorian University in Rome. On Jan 10, 1963, he was elected abbot of Mont-des-Cats, a position he held for thirty-five years until he retired in 1997. After his retirement, he embraced the eremitical life as a guest at the abbey of Sainte-Lioba at Simiane, a small town in Southern France. As his health failed, he returned to Mont-des-Cats, where in 2010 he died; he is buried there. During his lifetime, he was the general editor of the highly regarded theological journal *Collectanea Cisterciensia*, he served as moderator for our General Chapters, and he wrote numerous books, some of which were published by Cistercian Publications. His writings bring together his spiritual experience, which rises from a deep life of prayer, and his experience as part of a Cistercian monastic community.

I first met Dom André in Rome in 1971. We were together at many General Chapters of our Order and on various commissions. On one occasion I visited Mont-des-Cats. In June 1978 the Abbey of New Clairvaux hosted a symposium on the theme of Spiritual Fatherhood / Motherhood, at which Dom André presented a noteworthy paper entitled "Spiritual Fatherhood in the Literature of the Desert." He spoke of a spiritual father / mother as representing not age but "rather a ministry of wisdom at the center of the Christian community."[1]

Dom André was a monk, spiritual father, theologian, lecturer, author, translator, and friend. In the pages below Dom André's homilies on the Gospel passages read in year A of the church's three-year liturgical cycle appear in an elegant English translation by Br. Paul Rowe, OCSO; his homilies from years B and C will follow in subsequent volumes. All of these homilies faithfully reflect Dom André's spiritual insights and the fullness of his life experience. In them Dom André opens up for us the wisdom at the center of the Christian community and in the teachings of Christ. As a teacher and rabbi he ministers and reveals to us the mysteries of divinity. Contemplative reflection on these Gospel passages and on Dom André's insights will guide one's way of life into a deeper union with God.

Dom André titled this series of homilies *Heureuse Faiblesse*, translated here as *Blessed Weakness*. As his biographer Charles Wright explains, this phrase expresses a favorite

[1] André Louf, "Spiritual Fatherhood in the Literature of the Desert," trans. Monique Coyne, in *Abba: Guides to Wholeness and Holiness East and West. Papers Presented at a Symposium on Spiritual Fatherhood/Motherhood at the Abbey of New Clairvaux, Vina, California, 12–16 June 1978*, ed. John R. Sommerfeldt, Cistercian Studies Series 38 (Kalamazoo, MI: Cistercian Publications, 1978), 37–63, here 38.

theme of Dom André's: that as Jesus left behind his glory and became a man in weakness, living among and ministering to the poor, so he especially loves humans in their weakness. In his book Wright writes at some length on this point, saying that for Dom André, "Sin is a *felix culpa,* a happy fault, a chance for salvation. Through it and the repentance it allows, the merciful God reveals himself and becomes perceptible to the heart."[2]

As Wright points out, Dom André's teaching on this subject reflects an earlier Cistercian understanding:

> In Louf's eyes, taking up an idea dear to Saint Bernard, sin becomes part of mystical experience[3] and of divine pedagogy. God makes use of sin to proclaim his love and to reveal the superabundance of his mercy. "We might even say," [Louf] says, boldly, "that he has a need for the sin that has a share in the economy of salvation, since it detaches us . . .[4] from our pretending to build our own spiritual edifice with our own strength."[5] We think we can reach the Lord by the deployment of our own efforts, the display of our virtue, but it is our misery that activates his mercy. Sin is "the combustible fuel of love": from the very moment that it is revealed to us, it has already been pardoned.[6]

[2] Charles Wright, *The Way of The Heart*, trans. Brian Kerns, Monastic Wisdom series 72 (Collegeville, MN: Cistercian Publications, 2024), 137–41, here 137.

[3] See for example André Louf, "Bernard, Abbé," in *Bernard de Clairvaux: Histoire, mentalités, spiritualité*, Sources Chrétiennes 380 (Paris: Cerf, 1992), 371; and André Louf, "La faiblesse, un chemin pascal selon Saint Bernard," *Collectanea Cisterciensia* 65 (2003): 15–20.

[4] Dom André frequently, as here, uses ellipses to indicate a suspension in his words, a brief pause for reflection. Such ellipses in the body of this volume do not represent omissions by the homilies' editor or translator. Ellipses in this Foreword, however, indicate its author's omissions.

[5] André Louf, "La métanoïa, lieu de l'Esprit," unedited chapter talk at Mont-des-Cats, ADMC, Feb. 1971.

[6] Wright, *The Way of The Heart*, 139.

It is no wonder, then, that Dom André incorporates that perspective as a dominant theme while preaching to his community. Throughout the homilies included in this volume he calls attention to the identity between Jesus in his weakness and the various kinds of weakness manifested by those whom he came to save, as in his homily for the second Sunday of Advent:

> [Jesus] will be called a glutton and a drunkard, a friend of tax collectors and sinners (Matt 11:19), in short, not a respectable person. And there will be worse to come. One day, his family will come to seize him and remove him from public view, in order to protect him from himself, on the grounds that he is insane. . . . With Jesus, the sick are healed, the blind see, the lame walk, lepers are cleansed, the deaf hear, and even the dead are restored to life. In short, he directs his words preferentially to the poor, to whom the Gospel is announced. When God descends to visit human beings, it is to the poor that he goes. (12)

This early introduction of the theme evolves in different ways as the year progresses, recurring especially during Ordinary Time. On the fourth Sunday of Ordinary Time, preaching on the Beatitudes, Dom André speaks of human weakness not as he had earlier, as a matter of physical and mental incapacity, but of the internal hunger and thirst that men and women experience:

> It is as if the kingdom of Jesus cannot be glimpsed except through a certain hollow of human existence, through a void that is waiting to be filled, as if it were kept hidden behind a feeling of destitution, of need, that we fail to identify on the first attempt. As Jesus said, through a hunger and thirst for righteousness—that is, in biblical language, a still vague hunger and thirst for holiness. O happy poverty! (105)

He continues, now explaining that it is that void that allows to those who yearn a vision of the kingdom and that elicits Jesus' summons to them:

> Happy hunger and happy thirst, for which moreover Jesus offers us his felicitations, since in them there appear to us even now, in the form of a void, the future delights and refreshments of the kingdom. These mysterious voids in our life, sometimes experienced as acutely painful, yet accepted and offered up to God, become for each one of us the sure sign that the kingdom of Jesus is knocking at the door of our heart, and that we are among those made blessed by his call—that in addition discredits us in the eyes of a world that we were claiming to win for Christ. (106)

Later still, in the homily for the tenth Sunday of Ordinary Time, Dom André returns to this theme, now focusing on the human weakness of sin. He includes himself among his hearers, explaining that one must acknowledge such frailty if one is to know Jesus' love:

> Righteous people likewise fail to find favor with Jesus. He very quickly intuits that they basically feel no need of him. They consider themselves to be in good health. Are their lives not in order, precisely in view of their sacrifices? Why would they open themselves to something else, for example, to the love that Jesus came to bring? In reality, Jesus did not come for those who think themselves in order, but for those who have need of mercy. There was no other path by which Jesus could reach us. He does not meet us in our strength, but in our weakness, not in our virtues, but in our sin. . . . We must learn to content ourselves with this weakness in order to abide with delight in mercy. Every claim to perfection is superfluous here, even every ideal sanctity is out of place, and to display the face of the righteous would be to wear a mask that

> keeps us at a distance from Jesus, who prefers to sit at the table of sinners. (124–25)

Finally, remarkably, on the Sunday celebrating Christ the King, the last Sunday of the year, Dom André concludes the year's explication and proclamation of the Gospel of Matthew, one more time insisting that God became incarnate among and for the poverty stricken, the poor, the little ones. He ends by reminding his listeners—reminding us—that in our own weakness, hunger, and sin, we are rich, allowed to enter the kingdom if we recognize Jesus as himself one of the poor:

> From now on, there is no room for doubt: Jesus is now present among all the "least ones" whom he recognizes as his brothers and sisters. If they suffer hunger or thirst, if they are sick or persecuted and thrown into prison, it is Jesus who unites them to himself and appeals to us in their person (Matt 25:40). Our king is the brother of the lowly, he is close to those who call upon him. More than that: he and they are one. That is why the poor go before us into his kingdom (Matt 21:31), whereas we, the rich, can only follow them in the measure that we have been able to recognize him in them. (204)

In his preface to this collection Dom André wrote that although he originally addressed his homilies primarily to "his own brothers in monastic life," he expected that they would not appear "foreign" to the laity, those "immersed in the world" (3–4). Indeed in this volume almost nothing seems to apply exclusively to monks and nuns. While a few times he refers to a lesson read earlier that day, or he speaks of someone who has recently addressed the community, his preaching is always primarily concerned with the life of Christians, wherever and however they live. His repeated attention to Jesus' coming to the little ones of the world and Jesus' presence among those who struggle in their longing to know God is by no means a theme limited to those within the cloister.

One might also recognize as specific to monastic life the occasional references to vocations, a subject of particular concern to monks and nuns. But even these passages are of similarly great moment to people outside the monastery, for those who initially responded to Jesus' call—the women and fishermen and tax collectors and families gathered on the hillside—were not monks but ordinary people who upon hearing Jesus' word at once turned to him. As Dom André says of them, "The suddenness of such vocations never ceases to astonish us, and it even raises some questions. Few actions are as spontaneous as the response to Jesus' call in the gospels. No one reasons it out, no one weighs the pros and the cons, no one counts the cost. They simply leave everything and follow Jesus" (102). Today too, lay persons as well as monks hear Jesus' call and suddenly, surprisingly, follow him.

The first homily in this volume, preached on the first Sunday of Advent, is particularly clear in its implicit rebuke of all who hear or read it, lay as well as monastic. Its description of the heedlessness with which people move through their lives is so insistent (and so captivating in this expression) that its power reaches well beyond the monastery walls:

> He will come at the end of time, he will come at the hour of our death, and each time it will be a surprise, a happy surprise. But he also comes every day; he continually anticipates in the depths of our heart these two other advents. Alas, here too we are at risk of being taken by surprise. Surprised at the measure of our thoughtlessness, at the heedlessness in which we traverse the events of our lives, distracted, dissipated,

> living entirely on the surface of things, outside of ourselves, horribly extroverted and content to be so, and, consequently, deaf and insensible to the movement of the Spirit, to what Saint John calls its outpouring into our hearts (1 John 2:20-27), incapable of discerning therein the signs of Jesus' coming. And this again verifies what Jesus had predicted: it is always at the hour we do not expect that the Son of Man comes to us—and that, every day and at every instant. (7)

In the homily for Holy Thursday, on the meaning of the Eucharist, Dom André speaks to the community of Christians, all who receive and all who serve. He focuses first on the presence of Jesus among them, then reminds them of the way in which the Eucharist links past, present, and future:

> To celebrate the memorial of Jesus, however, is much more than piously to remember the past. The paschal memorial is, we could say, an extendable memorial. It not only commemorates the past, but it brings the past into the present. The memory of Jesus' past becomes the burning actuality of the church and of the world today. Jesus is present at the heart of the community that reenacts the Last Supper. He is also present among those who humbly serve their brothers and sisters. It is impossible to resemble him more closely than that: "I have given you an example to follow that, as I have done for you, you must also do." Impossible more efficaciously to reveal Jesus to the world: "By this all will know that you are my disciples, if you have love for one another" (John 13:35). . . . Not only does this memory bring the past into our today, but it also projects it into the future. It is a memory that anticipates, a memory that, being already a certitude today, is also hope for tomorrow. (57–58)

Dom André imbues all these homilies with the great images and themes of the Gospel—the wild olive tree of the Gentiles grafted onto the root of Judaism, feasts and wedding garments and insufficient oil, and God's carefully tended vineyard ravaged by greed and murder. Over and over he recalls the voice of Jesus, the presence of Jesus, the face of Jesus: "Since the moment of our baptism, we bear the features of Jesus' countenance stamped on our hearts. Not the exterior form of his visage, the color of his eyes or of his hair, but his true face, the eternal face of the Risen One from beyond this world" (80).

At the same time Dom André stamps each homily with his own style—active verbs and concrete nouns, an avoidance of abstraction, language familiar, engaging, and so all the more powerful. He often breaks off the movement of his sentences before quite finishing his thought, leading the reader forward while allowing the kicker, the punch line, to stand alone, a fragment of thought that emphasizes the essence of the point he wants to make and that the reader finds worth waiting for and then remembering.

The reader of these homilies cannot help but recognize in them the voice of a great preacher, a brilliant writer, a passionate follower of the Gospel, a man of God, and a fellow Christian. The opportunity to hear the words of the Gospel at the beginning of each homily and then to listen to Dom André open them up for understanding is a happy one.

Thomas X. Davis, OCSO
Abbey of New Clairvaux
Vina, California

# Blessed Weakness

# Preface

About fifteen years ago, under the title *Love Alone Suffices*, an initial collection of homilies for the Sundays of the three-year liturgical cycle (A, B, and C) saw the light of day. When the three volumes had subsequently gone out of stock and a second edition had been requested, the editor preferred that the readers be offered a new collection that would include the as-yet unedited homilies.

The homilies of the two collections have an identical origin. Each of them was composed and preached for an intended audience of monks who were customarily joined, above all on Sundays, by an assembly of laity. Nevertheless, it was principally his own brothers in monastic life whom the preacher addressed in the course of the dominical or festal celebrations. The monks' worries, their difficulties, and their temptations, no less than their hopes, find themselves there, confronted with the light and the strength released by God's Word. Thus these texts first constitute the echo of that interior journey proper to contemplatives, treating less directly the diverse questions of our age that never cease making appeal to a church irreducibly present at the heart of the world.

However, the light that these texts seek to reflect always finds its source in the words of Jesus himself. For this reason too, it can never show itself as foreign to the experience of those who are directly engaged in the myriad occupations of a life immersed in the world. If we scrutinize the secrets of the Gospel patiently, lovingly, Sunday after Sunday, we cannot help but touch the core of every Christian experience, be it the experience of those struggling with the world or of those who keep a certain distance from the world in monastic solitude. Besides, the latter is found to be equally at the heart of the world—in a different manner, of course, but no less efficaciously for all that. To let ourselves be grasped by the Word so that it may transform us into praise and intercession, or so that we may bear witness to it before our brothers and sisters—this presupposes, equally in both cases, an intimacy with the Word.

In either case, we will surely not long remain unaware of what perhaps constitutes the quintessence of all authentic Christian faith, of the only light that can enlighten us all along the way of faith—namely that the heights of divine love, to which God wills to direct us, would have us first of all entirely poor and stripped bare before then, in the divine tenderness, filling us with God's gifts and his joy. Rather than satiating us immediately beyond all that we would have dared imagine, God's joy begins by radically impoverishing us. This is something that sometimes takes us many years to understand, whether we find ourselves in the heart of the cloister or along the great highways of the world where we proclaim the Word, until one day we surrender and commend ourselves to an omnipotence that is well-pleased in our weakness.

Hence the title under which these texts are here gathered. It expresses one of the most striking evangelical intuitions of Saint Bernard of Clairvaux. He knew how to give it form in his own brilliant style, with deeply moving accents, in which he reproduced an echo of many texts of Scripture—a thunderous intuition to which the lives of countless saints, apostles, and mystics, have given moving testimony down the ages: O happy, blessed weakness!

## First Sunday of Advent

Matthew 24:37-44

*Jesus was speaking to his disciples about his coming: "At the coming of the Son of Man, it will be as it was in the days of Noah. In those days, before the flood, they were eating, drinking, and getting married up to the day when Noah entered the ark. They suspected nothing until the flood came and engulfed them all. So shall it be also at the advent of the Son of Man. Two men will be in the field: one will be taken, the other left. Two women will be at the mill: one will be taken, the other left. Keep watch, therefore! For you do not know the day when your Lord will come. Be sure of this, if the master of the house had known the hour when the thief was coming, he would have stayed awake and not let someone break into his house. In the same way, you too must be prepared. For, at an hour you do not expect, the Son of Man will come."*

When God comes to meet us, he surprises us. We weren't expecting him. Maybe we had never really expected him? Or we had expected him without believing too much, as with an event that is in any case unforeseeable and that it would be futile to count on. But, all of a sudden, there is God, catching us unawares!

So will it be with his coming at the end of time, Jesus has just told us. No one will appear to have given it a thought, much less prepared for it. The element of surprise will be total. People will be eating, drinking, and getting married as if nothing were going to happen, above all as if nothing were ever going to cease, as if the world were going to endure without end, always getting better and better, progressively making advances. "They did not suspect a thing," says Jesus, "until the flood came and engulfed them all." In the same way, Jesus will return amid a general heedlessness.

At all events, we might suppose that the end of time, should it ever arrive, will not concern us. Although history has known epochs haunted by fear of an imminent final cataclysm, that does not appear to be the preponderant anxiety of our age. We dream instead of unlimited progress, not of catastrophes that would end everything.

There will be, of course, our personal end, our own death, that other coming of Jesus, a personal advent, that involves only himself and each one of us. We know that it is ineluctable and that, besides, nothing is more unpredictable. We know this with our reason, but has it really penetrated our hearts? We are not at all astonished to have survived thus far, whereas so many others, often much younger than we, have long since crossed over to the other side. At bottom, we too are living in complete insouciance, as if death principally concerned others, as if the fact of still being here were an acquired right, almost an entitlement.

And nevertheless, even if the hour of our death remains distant, it is at the same time already close at hand. It draws closer with the passing of every hour. It can cast a disquieting shadow over our life, awaken ancestral fears, but it can also inundate us with light, evoke in us a great feeling of assurance and an ardent thirst—a thirst for the encounter. Because every day? Hour? Moment? that passes can be, and fundamentally is, a missed rendezvous with Jesus, a meeting postponed, an appointment deferred. And what an appointment!

This is what Jesus really wants to tell us when he exhorts us to keep vigil, since we do not know the day when he will come: not to keep watch with anxiety or terror, but in the joy of an immense desire. To keep watch while waiting for someone is to express concretely the extent to which that person is awaited and to anticipate already—even to hasten on as far as possible—the hour of meeting. To keep watch as we wait for Jesus, in forgetfulness of the things of the world that will inevitably pass away one day, is to tell him that we love him as the most precious treasure of our life.

He will come at the end of time, he will come at the hour of our death, and each time it will be a surprise, a happy surprise. But he also comes every day; he continually anticipates in the depths of our heart these two other advents. Alas, here too we are at risk of being taken by surprise. Surprised at the measure of our thoughtlessness, at the heedlessness in which we traverse the events of our lives, distracted, dissipated, living entirely on the surface of things, outside of ourselves, horribly extroverted and content to be so, and, consequently, deaf and insensible to the movement of the Spirit, to what Saint John calls its outpouring into our hearts (1 John 2:20-27), incapable of discerning therein the signs of Jesus' coming. And this again verifies what Jesus had predicted: it is always at the hour we do not expect that the Son of Man comes to us—and that, every day and at every instant.

# Second Sunday of Advent

Matthew 3:1-12

*In those days, John the Baptist appeared in the desert, proclaiming "Repent, for the kingdom of heaven is at hand!" It was John who was designated by the word that came through the prophet Isaiah: "A voice cries out in the desert: 'Prepare the way of the Lord, make straight his paths!'" John wore a tunic of camel's hair, with a leather belt around his waist. His food was locusts and wild honey. At that time, Jerusalem, all Judea, and the whole region around the Jordan came to him to be baptized by him in the Jordan River as they acknowledged their sins.*

*When he saw a great number of Pharisees and Sadducees coming to this baptism, he said to them "You brood of vipers! Who warned you to flee from the coming wrath? Produce good fruits as evidence of your repentance, and do not presume to say to yourselves 'We have Abraham for our father.' For I tell you that God can raise up children to Abraham from these stones. The axe is already laid at the root of the trees: every tree that does not bear good fruit will be cut down and thrown into the fire. I baptize you with water unto repentance. But there is one coming after me who is mightier than I, and I am not worthy to unfasten his sandals. He will baptize you with the Holy Spirit and with fire; the winnowing fan is in his hand to clear his threshing floor and gather the wheat into his barn. But the chaff he will burn with unquenchable fire."*

A baptism is only a beginning. It presupposes a sequel throughout the whole of one's life, an unfolding.

As John the Baptist baptizes people in the Jordan, he is aware of this. His baptism is provisional, merely the initiation of conversion. It calls for a fulfillment that it cannot provide. John is the point of completion of the Old Covenant, and he must await another, halted as he is at the border of the New Covenant yet unable to enter it alone.

He can only proclaim that the old world is coming to an end, that the kingdom is at hand, that one mightier than he is about to make his appearance, and that his own baptism will receive from the one who is to come its expected supplement: a baptism in the Holy Spirit and fire.

For the Jews of that time, to plunge into the Jordan and rise up again was symbolically to reenact the triumphal entrance of the chosen people into the Promised Land, when the waters of the Jordan withdrew so that the Israelites could cross it dry-shod. For Jesus to cross the Jordan in turn is to anticipate his own passage from death to resurrection and, at the same time, to establish what will become after him, in the church, the sacrament of Christian baptism, the baptism that we have received and that makes us enter into death with Jesus so that we might live from his new life.

However, for the Christian also the sacrament of baptism, albeit infinitely more efficacious than that of John the Baptist, is still only a beginning. As a sign of the Passover of Jesus, this baptism contains all the reality thereof, but only in the form of a seed. Such a seed includes simultaneously the promise of flowers and fruits and the real capacity to produce them one day. All the vital energy is already present in the seed, but fragile, threatened, and yet unforeseeable.

One day, all will come to pass, namely, the glorious and transfigured life of Jesus risen among us. But all, while still in progress, can also be compromised. The debut of life can wilt, regress, suffocate, and finally be extinguished. It is a life that unceasingly brushes against death. It is for this reason that Christian baptism, even if it already contains everything in hope, also needs a completion. Christians await from the one who is to come, from Jesus, a second baptism in the Holy Spirit and in fire.

But what does that mean? Certainly it is undeniable that through baptism our faults have been forgiven, we have been grafted onto Jesus, and divine life has inoculated us. We believe this. At the same time, however, we feel that our old wounds leave scars that could all too easily reopen and bleed anew. The life of Jesus has not yet totally invested our psychological constitution or durably transformed our habits or finally transfigured our bodies. Far from it. All our days we suffer from this condition, and we look for something more, a new baptism in the Holy Spirit and fire.

The fire demands flammable material to consume. This is the chaff of which Jesus speaks in the Gospel, chaff that hides the wheat. This is the dross that prevents the gold from appearing if the ore is spared the crucible. Chaff and dross: that is, everything within us that has not yet been invaded and transfigured by the life of Jesus and the power of the Spirit.

The forms of this new baptism are various. Most often, they take on the contours of our trials, of temptation under a thousand guises. Whatever they may be, our temptations are always Jesus in person, holding the winnowing fan in his hand that he may retain only the good grain. These temptations are, in any case, provisional, as we wait for that ultimate baptism that is our death, the decisive trial and final purification by the Spirit and fire, at the threshold of our meeting with him who will finally be there.

# Third Sunday of Advent

Matthew 11:2-11

*From his place in prison, John the Baptist heard of what Christ was doing. He sent some of his disciples to him with the question "Are you the one who is to come, or are we to look for another?"*

*Jesus said to them in reply, "Go and tell John what you hear and see: the blind regain their sight, the lame walk, lepers are cleansed, the deaf hear, the dead are raised, and the poor have the Good News preached to them. And blessed are they who are not scandalized by me!"*

*When John's emissaries departed, Jesus began to speak to the crowds about John, saying "What did you go out to the desert to see? A reed swayed by the wind? . . .*[1] *Then, what did you go out to see? Someone dressed in fine clothing? But those dressed in fine clothing live in royal palaces. Then what did you go out to see? A prophet? Yes, I tell you, and more than a prophet. This is the one of whom it is written, 'Behold, I am sending my messenger ahead of you, to prepare the way before you.' Amen, I say to you, among those born of women, there is none greater than John the Baptist, but the least in the kingdom of heaven is greater than he."*

[1] Dom André frequently, as here, uses ellipses to indicate a suspension in his words, a brief pause for reflection. Except in the Foreword, such ellipses in this volume do not represent omissions by the homilies' editor or translator.

But who then is Jesus? How can he be recognized? And why is there always this doubt surrounding him—in our own day, to be sure, but also already among his contemporaries? Even John the Baptist, after having previously announced his coming, now seems gripped by this doubt. He sends some of his disciples to ask him, "Are you the one who is to come, or are we to look for another?"

Elsewhere in the gospels, the same questions are raised, always about the identity of Jesus (Matt 16:14), and the opinions diverge. Some say that he is a prophet, others that he is Elijah; later, people will believe him to be John the Baptist raised from the dead (Matt 14:2). Certain designations are less flattering: he will be called a glutton and a drunkard, a friend of tax collectors and sinners (Matt 11:19), in short, not a respectable person. And there will be worse to come. One day, his family will come to seize him and remove him from public view, in order to protect him from himself, on the grounds that he is insane: "He is out of his mind" (Mark 3:21).

Could such a controversial figure be "the One who is to come," that is, the expected Messiah? To disclose his identity, Jesus applies to himself a text of Isaiah that describes the messianic times. His titles have nothing to do with an illustrious birth, nor with money or power. Neither does Jesus emerge from one of the Great Schools of his time. Like John the Baptist, he does not dress in luxurious garments or live in royal palaces.

Since he does not issue from the higher echelons of society, neither is his activity of any interest to them at first. On the contrary, it is aimed at a very particular social reality. With Jesus, the sick are healed, the blind see, the lame walk, lepers are cleansed, the deaf hear, and even the dead are restored to life. In short, he directs his words preferentially to the poor, to whom the Gospel is announced. When God descends to visit human beings, it is to the poor that he goes.

There is a trace of this divine preference in Jesus' customary vocabulary. He likes to speak of what is little and of little ones. Among the latter, he is visibly at ease. To enter into the kingdom, there is a single, indispensable condition: to become like a little child (Luke 18:17). The group of his disciples on whom the Father is bestowing this kingdom, and which will become the church, is in no way impressive or called to become so. Jesus calls it the "little flock" (Luke 12:32), which, for all its littleness, has nothing to fear. Besides, being little is almost sufficient in itself, but best of all, if possible, is to be "the least," because in the kingdom, it is the least who is the greatest (Luke 7:28). And that, not only because there the norms are turned completely upside down, but because he himself identifies with the least: "What you have done to these least brothers or sisters of mine, that you have done to me" (Matt 25:40). Amid his disciples, Jesus is not only the one who serves, but even the least one and recognizable among all the littlest ones. And when Jesus, in the gospel that we have just heard, calls John the Baptist the greatest among those born of women, only to add that the least in the kingdom of heaven is greater than he, some exegetes think that he is talking about himself and that he is greater than John the Baptist simply because he himself is the least. In so saying, Jesus would have fully adopted and made his own a sobriquet—"the least"—that his adversaries had coined to ridicule him in the eyes of the crowd.

Well, here is Jesus acquiescing in, and applying to himself, the sobriquet. Yes indeed, his only ambition is to be the least. And it is precisely by this trait, this surprising littleness, that he can be recognized. For when God comes to visit his people, he thus clothes himself in poverty and so conceals himself in what is littlest that he can only be recognized as God by the one who welcomes him in this guise, as infinitely, ridiculously little in human eyes.

# Fourth Sunday of Advent

## Matthew 1:18-24

*This is how the birth of Jesus Christ came about. When his mother Mary was betrothed to Joseph, but before they came together, she was found to be with child through the Holy Spirit. Joseph, her husband, who was a righteous man, did not want to denounce her publicly but decided to divorce her quietly. He had made up his mind to do this when, behold, the angel of the Lord appeared to him in a dream and said to him, "Joseph, son of David, do not be afraid to take Mary, your wife, into your home. For the child that has been conceived in her comes from the Holy Spirit. She will bring forth a son, and you will name him Jesus (that is, 'the Lord saves'), for he will save his people from their sins."*

*All this took place to fulfill what was spoken by the Lord through the prophet: "Behold, the Virgin will conceive and bear a son, and they shall name him Emmanuel," which is translated, "God is with us."*

*When Joseph awoke, he did as the angel of the Lord had commanded and took his wife into his home.*

The most precious fruit on earth is that to which a woman gives birth: the child, a human being in miniature, a sheer miracle of God. She does not fashion it by herself, nor could she. Another must intervene, her husband, who will give her the wherewithal to produce such a fruit in a union and embrace of love, the reflection of another love in whose image the two were created in the beginning: "In his image and likeness he created them, male and female he created them" (Gen 1:26).

Ever since then, through this image of himself, God is intensely present in every act of love, at every conception, and at every birth. Every couple, without knowing it, assumes this love of God, reflects it, and makes it fertile on earth. No one can love truly except in God, for God is love (1 John 4:8).

If God is present at all conceptions and at all births, he is thus present more particularly at some of them that were unexpected, unhoped for, and that, humanly speaking, ought never to have happened. This is especially true where the child to be born, from a woman who is barren or past the age of childbearing, will go on to play a role in the history of the chosen people. From Isaac, born of Sarah, to John the Baptist, born of Elizabeth, God has wished to show just how much these conceptions and births matter to him, being always the work of his love confided to the bodies of men and of women, but of women hitherto considered unfit.

But when God decides to cause his own Son to be born here below, his intervention, being all the more miraculous, will prove more insistent than ever. For the seed and breath of man could not suffice to engender within the body of the future mother the one who will be at once man and God. That the Word of God may truly be born here, it will require the intervention of the breath of God himself, his Holy Spirit. The Son of God could not have another father on earth, nor a mother who was not a virgin. This is what the angel has told us in the Gospel: "What has been conceived in Mary, your wife, comes from the Holy Spirit." The same thing that Gabriel had said to Mary herself, in Luke's story of the annunciation, at the moment when she seems ready to beg off and demur by declaring to him her intention to remain a virgin: "The Holy Spirit will come upon you and the power of the Most High will overshadow you; therefore the child will be holy and will be called Son of God" (Luke 1:35).

If every newly conceived or newborn child is a marvelous gift of God and reminds us a little of his paternity over all that exists, as well as of his unlimited love for human beings, the child Jesus will be more than a mere reflection of this love: he will be this love itself, God in person, Emmanuel, God with us. Not a distant and solitary love, however infinite, but a love of extraordinary proximity, a nuptial love with which God truly assumes and espouses our human nature, a love that makes of each human being a privileged and preferred beloved one of God.

This is the meaning of the name that the angel has just revealed to Joseph so that he might bestow it on the child on behalf of the unique Father, who is God: Jesus, that is, Savior. And the angel explains it: "For he will save his people from their sins." An eternally inexplicable excess of love that Christmas will grant us to relive: the Son of God has become man, not among saints but in the company of sinners. He has chosen for his bride neither the most beautiful nor the most perfect, but her who has been disfigured by her own straying. And he has done this, quite simply, to save her, that is, to love her to the end, to swallow up her sins in mercy, to reconcile her to himself and, according to the words of Saint Paul, to present her to himself "a glorious bride, without spot or wrinkle, henceforth holy and immaculate" (Eph 5:27).

# Christmas

## Luke 2:1-14

*In those days, a decree went out from Caesar Augustus that the whole world should be enrolled. This was the first enrollment, when Quirinius was governor of Syria. And everyone went to be enrolled, each to his own town. Joseph too went up from Nazareth in Galilee to Judea, to the city of David that is called Bethlehem—since he was of the house and family of David—there to be enrolled together with Mary, his wife, who was with child. While they were there, the time came for her to give birth to her child. And she gave birth to her firstborn son: she wrapped him in swaddling clothes and laid him in a manger, for there was no room for them in the inn.*

*Now there were shepherds in that district, dwelling in the fields and keeping the night watch over their flocks. Behold, the angel of the Lord appeared to them, and the glory of the Lord shone round about them. They were seized with great fear, but the angel said to them, "Fear not, for I come to proclaim to you good news of great joy for all the people. For today, in the city of David, a Savior has been born for you who is Christ and Lord. And behold, this is the sign that has been given you: you will find an infant wrapped in swaddling clothes and lying in a manger."*

*And suddenly, there was with the angel a great multitude of the heavenly host praising God and saying, "Glory to God in the highest heavens and peace on earth to the human race whom he loves."*

"I proclaim to you great joy that will be for all the people: a Savior has been born for us." These words of the angel to the shepherds have reverberated through the liturgy even unto our own assembly. And these words were but an echo of the announcement heard from the prophet Isaiah in the first reading: "You have made them exult with great exultation, as they rejoice before you as at the harvest, as men make merry when dividing the spoils."

This joy is indeed what we are accustomed to wish one another, in all the languages of Western Europe, on the occasion of this celebration: "Merry Christmas" [*Joyeux Noel*]. Though it may be night, or cold, or raining or snowing outside—or in our hearts—the birth of Jesus on earth brings to each one of us as it were a little gleam of light, a humble intimation of joy, even to those of us who are completely ignorant of the meaning of the feast. Christmas is for all a symbol of light, of warmth, and of joy, diametrically opposed to what nature spontaneously suggests to us at this time of year.

For us who have received the grace to know and to believe, there is in fact no greater joy than this encounter between God and human beings, than this bodily union between the Son of God and our humanity. There the whole of human nature finds itself welcoming the Son of God as a brother into the bosom of humanity; all human beings are henceforth destined to penetrate into the inner life of God. Christmas opens a door that leads into the heart of the Trinity.

For the birth of Jesus from the womb of the Virgin Mary is a prolongation, in time and on earth, of another birth quite anterior to this one, a continual birth, in eternity and heaven, from the bosom of the Father. And the joy of Mary and of Joseph, like that of the shepherds, is a reflection of the infinite joy that is the communion of the Father and the Son, in the unity of the Holy Spirit. The Father unceasingly contemplates the Son flowing out from the abyss of his love, and the Son perpetually returns the Father's gaze. A love that pronounces a Word and begets a Son, and a Son who welcomes the gift of his Father with an eternally loving thankfulness. Never in a million years, not even on this night, could a mortal creature presume to calculate the dimensions of this divine joy.

Nevertheless, now every human being is called to enter in turn into this joy, to share at least a few crumbs of it, and even, day by day, to increase one's portion. Our vocation as baptized persons has no other meaning than this: that this joy of the Father and of the Son that was also, albeit more modestly, the joy of the Virgin Mary on this Christmas night—that this joy may become progressively our own. Because we too are henceforth sons and daughter in the only Son, coheirs with him. We can cry out with him, "Abba, Father," in the Holy Spirit, since he is no longer Jesus' Father alone but also, and truly, our Father (Rom 8:15).

The birth that took place on Christmas night and that takes place anew in this liturgy is thus the prolongation of the eternal birth within the Trinity. But it gains a new prolongation in the depth of our heart that has now become a new dwelling place of Jesus, a Temple of the Spirit, a place of origins where the Father unceasingly engenders his Son, and each of us with him. From now on, the Christmas crèche is in our hearts, the bosom of the Father as well. It is there that we can welcome and adore the one who is reborn at every moment, and with him we can, with loving gratitude, contemplate the Father's face. It is there too that our joy finds its home, today and always. Yes: "Merry Christmas!"

# Feast of the Holy Family

Matthew 2:13-23

*After the visit of the Magi, the angel of the Lord appeared to Joseph in a dream saying, "Rise, take the child and his mother and flee to Egypt. Stay there until I tell you, for Herod is going to search for the child to destroy him." So Joseph arose, took the child and his mother by night, and withdrew into Egypt, where he remained until the death of Herod. Thus was fulfilled what the Lord had spoken through the prophet: "Out of Egypt I called my son."*

*After the death of Herod, the angel of the Lord appeared to Joseph in a dream and said to him, "Rise, take the child and his mother, and go back to the land of Israel, for those who sought the child's life are dead." Joseph arose, took the child and his mother, and returned to the land of Israel. But when he heard that Archelaus was ruling in Judea in place of his father, Herod, he was afraid to return there. And having been warned in a dream, he withdrew to the region of Galilee and went to live in a town called Nazareth, that what the Lord had spoken through the prophets might be fulfilled: "He shall be called a Nazarene."*

"He came to his own, and his own did not receive him" (John 1:11). This word of the Apostle John is verified from

Jesus' first days on earth. Of royal lineage, the Son of David, he more than anyone, should have been at home in Israel. Alas! Scarcely had he taken possession of his territory than he was compelled to flee in secret. Someone in whom he had inspired rivalry and fear was seeking his life. He in turn was recapitulating the experience of his ancestors: dwelling in exile in a foreign land, Egypt.

It was a provisional stay, in any case. A short time later, Joseph again took to the road to restore Jesus to his own country—with circumspection, however: with Herod's son ruling over Judea, it was more prudent to pass unnoticed into Galilee.

When God comes down to earth, he confronts a hostile world. He comes to save human beings, but they want to get rid of him. He offers forgiveness and love, but this elicits mistrust and fear that will continually increase until they finally issue in that hatred, blind and massive, that leads Jesus to his definitive expulsion—on the cross.

"His own did not receive him." At the heart of this world of rejection, however, God had prepared for his Son a harbor of welcome, an oasis of peace and of gentleness: Mary, his mother, Joseph, the husband of Mary, who will be like a father to him—the Holy Family. Every child coming into the world has the right to such a cradle, to arms that cradle it with love and with nurturing tenderness, so that it may survive. Jesus had need of it more than others, even if his vulnerability was of a different nature. For the divine power that inhabited him could not help but unleash against itself the power of evil. Basically, he was weaker in the measure that he was stronger, just as one day he would be all the stronger as he became weaker. More dangerously exposed than anyone else, Jesus first needed parents, then a circle of disciples and friends.

The same can be said today of Jesus at the heart of his church. Of course, by his Passover, he has once and for all conquered the world and the powers of evil. The latter nevertheless continue to vegetate for the duration. They can frighten Jesus' disciples, simulating failures, feigning regressions, counteracting some defeats. His church comes out of these confrontations apparently enfeebled, even threatened with death and extinction.

As Jesus recalled, "The disciple is not above his Master. If they have hated me, they will hate you also" (Luke 6:40). And if, before us, Jesus had to reenact the experience of exile in a foreign land, his church also always courts the risk of being cast off to the margins of respectable society or to those of society as a whole, to the outskirts of the world. And she too is unable to survive without a haven of peace and rest, without a hearth of love and tenderness, without a Holy Family—a Family that is constituted day after day around Jesus, present in its midst: "I will be with you, to the end of the time" (Matt 28:20); "Take courage, I have conquered the world" (John 16:33). These are two of Jesus' sayings upon which the church can ceaselessly depend.

Mary is also present in this family: discreet, silent, but always active with it as she was at the wedding of Cana, and beneath the cross, and in the upper room at the hour of Pentecost: a presence of infinite tenderness and ardent supplication.

Joseph too is present here, with those in the family whose charge it is to guide their brothers and sisters, like Peter, the first believer, upon whose faith the church is built, and, along with him, a cloud of innumerable witnesses of all times who nourish her faith down to this day. If his own did not receive Jesus, his little flock did, in the name of everyone else, the little flock to whom it has pleased the Father to give the kingdom (Luke 12:32). A pinch of yeast mixed into the world's dough (Luke 13:21), so that it might one day cause the whole world to rise up to its meeting with Jesus.

# Epiphany

## Matthew 2:1-12

*Jesus was born in Bethlehem of Judea in the days of King Herod the Great. Now behold, Magi came from the East and arrived in Jerusalem asking, "Where is the newborn king of the Jews? We saw his star at its rising and have come to do him homage." When he heard this, King Herod was greatly shaken, and all Jerusalem with him. He assembled all the chief priests and scribes of Israel and inquired of them where the Messiah was to be born. They said in reply, "In Bethlehem of Judea, for thus it has been written through the prophet: 'and you, Bethlehem in Judah, are by no means least among the leading districts of Judah, for from you will come a ruler who will shepherd my people Israel.'" Then Herod called the Magi in secret to ascertain from them the time of the star's appearance. And sending them on to Bethlehem, he said to them, "Go, search diligently for the child, and when you have found him, send me word, that I too may go and do him homage." When the king finished speaking, they departed.*

*And behold, the star that they had seen at its rising preceded them until it came to rest over the place where the child was. They were overjoyed at seeing the star, and on entering the house, they found the child with Mary his mother. They did him homage and, opening their treasures, offered him gifts of gold, frankincense, and myrrh. And having been warned in a dream not to return to Herod, they departed to their own country by another way.*

According to Luke, Jesus is first manifested to some shepherds, not to the leaders or priests of his people. According to Matthew, in the Gospel that we just heard, it is no longer even to members of his own people that he is shown, but to strangers, to magi who have come from the East. When God becomes man, he is not immediately visible to just anyone. He has his preferences, and he honors them: they are the most dispossessed and those afar off.

Isaiah had announced it, as the first reading reminds us: Jerusalem will receive a multitude of new sons and daughters who will come to her from distant lands. As we celebrate today the feast of the Epiphany, that is to say of the Manifestation of Jesus, we think spontaneously of those scarcely evangelized nations to whom the good news is also addressed and whom we intend to honor today in the person of the three magi-kings.

We are not mistaken in doing so, but we are not exactly right either, because our memory thus proves itself a bit defective. The magi who come from afar to discover Jesus are not in the first instance the Africans or Orientals who must receive the Gospel. They are first of all we ourselves, who once had no part in the chosen people, we who may be Gaulois, Teutons, Anglo-Saxons, Batavians, and even Romans, all foreigners and barbarians in the eyes of the Jews who form the root.

Maybe this occurred to you the other day when Cardinal Lustiger spoke to you, himself an authentic Jew but who, like the first disciples of Jesus, has recognized the Messiah from his Jewish identity. He belongs carnally to Jesus' race; he is truly at home in Jesus' church. He is a child of the household. He never had to be engrafted like us, like a wild branch onto the noble olive tree. He forms part of the root, and in becoming Christian he has remained a Jew all the more, a Jew of the truest sort. The foreigners, immigrants, savages—that's us, and it is by an unheard-of mercy that we have been allowed to take our place at the heart of the chosen people. Epiphany is first of all our own feast. It should be for us an occasion for ceaseless thanksgiving.

Here is the Mystery hidden in God and made known today "through the mouth of the holy apostles and prophets" whom Paul evokes in the second reading. In the Epistle to the Ephesians, Saint Paul spells it out more precisely: "You are no longer strangers and aliens; you are fellow citizens [compatriots] of the saints [that is, of the Jewish people] and members of the family of God" (Eph 2:19). Henceforth there can be no doubt: we find ourselves on an equal footing with the other members of the chosen people, we share in all their privileges, we are chosen on the same basis as they, and, if I dare to say so, we are as much Jews as the other Jews. Thanks be to God.

But all this comes to us first of all thanks to Jesus Christ, to his birth among us, recognized equally by those who were close at hand—the Jewish shepherds—as by those who were far off—the magi of the Orient—thanks above all to his death and resurrection. It is again Saint Paul who explains this to us: "Now, you who once were far off have been brought near through the blood of Christ. It is he who is our peace, uniting what was divided. In his own flesh, he has destroyed the barrier of enmity that kept us apart" (Eph 2:14-15).

It is he, Jesus, who is our peace, the same peace that the angels came to announce on Christmas night, not only to the Jewish people but to all human beings beloved by God. This peace that today reigns in our hearts is the reflection of our joy at belonging henceforth, in our turn, to the chosen people, and at feeling that we have gained a heart of immense solidarity, of universal brotherhood and sisterhood, a heart that lives and intercedes not only for the chosen people, but for all "human beings beloved by God" (Luke 2:14), as we ourselves have been loved by him.

# Baptism of Jesus

Matthew 3:13-17

*Jesus, arriving from Galilee, appeared at the banks of the Jordan and came to John to be baptized by him. John tried to prevent him, saying, "It is I who need to be baptized by you, but you come to me!" Jesus said in reply, "Allow it for now, for thus it is fitting for us to fulfill all righteousness." So John allowed it.*

*As soon as Jesus had been baptized, he came up out of the water. And behold, the heavens were opened, and he saw the Spirit of God descend and come upon him in the form of a dove. And from the heavens, a voice was saying, "This is my beloved Son. In him I have placed all my love!"*

The baptism that Jesus has just received is different from that which the Jews received at the banks of the same Jordan, from the hands of the same John the Baptist. For the Jews, the baptism was a matter of conversion. For Jesus, it was like a new birth, in which was suddenly revealed, to his ears and to his heart, the mysterious plenitude of the depths of his being: he was beyond any doubt a man, but also, and at the same time, the Son of the Father and God himself.

It was a solemn and grave moment in his life as a man. Several years earlier, Jesus had crossed the threshold of manhood. He has just taken a decisive step: he has left his parental home and launched upon his public life. It is now, at this moment when he is carrying out a familiar rite with his fellow Jews, that the mystery is suddenly unveiled before him.

Like the others, Jesus has stripped off his clothes and proceeds in the splendor of his nakedness, far more glorious than the bystanders are able to perceive. But in the form of baptism, it is the Spirit of God whom he receives and who comes to rest upon him, while at the same time a voice resounds—the voice of the Father who comes once and for all to touch and wound his human heart: "This is my beloved Son; in him I have placed all my love!"

Nothing was ever more precarious or, at the same time, more solemn and grave than this declaration of great love. But also, never was a declaration of love on earth more uplifting, more sweetly intoxicating than that which Jesus received on the morning of his baptism, into a heart as transparent as crystal, with total availability and complete consent.

Not that this word of love was, strictly speaking, a surprise for Jesus. From all eternity, he knew this love and this word. And it is too little to say that he knew them. It is better to say that Jesus was himself, at the deepest level of his being, this word of love: the Word in which the Father never ceases to express the plenitude of his tenderness, and that from all eternity.

If today there is a surprise for the ears and heart of Jesus, it is because this word of love is expressed, for the first time, in human language and addressed to a human being, Jesus of Nazareth—but a human being in whom dwells the fullness of divinity. It is in this that the Father's word is absolutely new and thus must have radically unsettled Jesus, once and for all. How was a man, how was human nature going to be able to bear the weight and the ardor of such a love? The whole life of Jesus, his death and resurrection included, will come to respond to this question.

For once unleashed on the earth, this word of the Father is forever inexhaustible and never ceases to resound here. First in the heart of Jesus, who, thanks to this word, could pass through his human life even to the point of drinking the cup that the Father had prepared for him. But the echo of this word of love continues to sound even to this day in the hearts of all those who have recognized in Jesus the Son of God, and in whom the Spirit incessantly murmurs "Abba, Father" (Rom 8:15). This is the only word of love that is really worth the trouble and that is stammered laboriously in all our terrestrial loves, so glorious and at the same time wounded, that find their eternal source and appeasement in the reciprocal love of the Father and the Son.

# Ash Wednesday

## Matthew 6:1-18

*When the disciples had gathered around Jesus on the mountain, he said to them, "If you want to live in the way of the righteous, avoid acting so as to get people to notice you. Otherwise, you will have no reward from your Father in heaven. Therefore, when you give alms, do not blow a trumpet before you as do the hypocrites in the synagogues and in the streets, so that they might receive praise from others. Amen, I say to you, they have had their reward. But when you give alms, do not let your left hand know what your right hand is doing, so that your almsgiving may be secret. And your Father, who sees in secret, will repay you.*

*"When you pray, do not be like the hypocrites, who love to stand praying in synagogues and on street corners so that others will notice them. Amen, I say to you, they have had their reward. But when you pray, go to your inner room, shut the door, and pray to your Father in secret. And your Father, who sees in secret, will repay you.*

*"When you fast, do not adopt a gloomy appearance, as the hypocrites do: they wear a downcast look so that others will know they are fasting. Amen, I say to you: they have had their reward. But when you fast, anoint your head and wash your face, so that your fasting may be hidden except to your Father. And your Father, who sees what is hidden, will repay you."*

◈

"When you fast, anoint your head and wash your face." Jesus calls us to enter Lent as we would enter a feast, in a spirit of joy. This is not a self-evident approach. The idea of a somewhat prolonged period of fasting has nothing of itself to commend rejoicing. It is normal that we engage it with a bit of apprehension. Will I be able to maintain it? It will be all the easier to discontinue if our courage begins to flag and to find a thousand and one reasons to desist midway through Lent, or even before. No, at first glance, it is not gaiety of heart that will condition how we appear as we fast.

Yet it is important that it be so, that at a given moment courage may seem to be wanting to us. In fact, fasting reaches down into the unplumbed depths of our being. Not only because hunger is never agreeable to us but, much more seriously, because fasting touches and assaults us within that so mysterious, sometimes unspeakable, universe of our desires. And such an assault cannot but strike fear into us and cause us pain.

And this is fortunate, because it is indeed only on this condition that fasting can access within us, beneath the fear, another desire provisionally buried beneath our fears and awaken it: a desire that is the desire of the Holy Spirit within us, the very life of him who is in himself overflowing and infinite joy.

This joy is, however, provisionally buried within our fear and concealed by it. Whoever refuses to pass through this fear will never find this joy. That is the law of all life coming to birth, life in the Spirit not excepted. Jesus pronounced this law with the help of an image: "When a woman is in labor, she is in agony because her hour has come. But when she has given birth, she is overcome with joy because a new human being has been brought into the world" (John 16:12).

Thanks to God, she has not sought to avoid the sufferings of pregnancy, without which the child would have been stillborn.

Lent does not invite us to hide the inevitable suffering of the new life that must be born in us at Easter. It is a patient passage, through our apprehensions and our desires, to the search for the desire of the Holy Spirit who is hidden in the depths of our heart, a pilgrimage to spiritual joy.

That is why Lent demands a festive air, a face radiating joy. Recall that Saint Benedict desires that whatever specific offerings we make to God on this occasion be made "in the joy of the Holy Spirit." And every renunciation we make of our habitual inclinations, our superficial desires, I cite again, "food, drink, sleep, chatting, joking," he asks that we do so as we look forward "to holy Easter with joy and spiritual desire" (RB 49).

# First Sunday of Lent

## Matthew 4:1-11

*After he had been baptized, Jesus was led into the desert by the Spirit to be tempted by the devil. He fasted forty days and forty nights, and afterwards he was hungry. The tempter approached him and said, "If you are the Son of God, command that these stones become loaves of bread." But Jesus said in reply, "It is written, 'Not by bread alone does man live, but by every word that comes forth from the mouth of God.'"*

*Then the devil took him to the holy city, Jerusalem, and placed him on the parapet of the Temple, saying, "If you are the Son of God, cast yourself down; for it is written, 'For you he will command his angels, to bear you upon their hands lest you strike your foot against a stone.'" Jesus said to him, "It is also written, 'You shall not put the Lord, your God, to the test.'"*

*Then the devil took him to the top of a very high mountain and showed him all the kingdoms of the world in their glory, and he said to him, "All these I shall give you, if you prostrate yourself and worship me." And Jesus said to him, "Depart from me, Satan! For it is written, 'The Lord, your God, shall you worship and him alone shall you serve.'"*

*Then the devil departed from him. And behold, angels came and ministered to him.*

Here are two stories that have opposite endings. When Adam is tempted, Paradise becomes a desert producing thorns. With the temptation of Jesus, the desert is transformed into a Paradise populated by angels. Between these two temptations unfolds the whole history of salvation, to which Paul gives us the key in the second reading: "Just as through the disobedience of one man death came into the world, so through the obedience of one man came justification that gives life."

What has taken place between the two stories? At the time of the first temptation, a man succumbed and dragged the human race down with him. The second time, another man came out unscathed, communicating life to all his brothers and sisters. The second man, Jesus, was like the first in all things, with this addition: that he was the true Son of God, sent by his Father to take up anew the history of the first man, a history that no other man, left to his own resources, would be able to rewrite.

To take up anew the path of Adam was, for Jesus, to clothe himself with all the human fragility that was Adam's and, necessarily, to be himself exposed in turn to temptation. It was necessary, says the Epistle to the Hebrews, that Jesus, being equally as human as the rest of us, should be likewise tempted in all things (Heb 4:15). There where the first man had fallen, where the history of God's marvels had been cut short and had, for centuries, deviated from the trajectory that the Father had at first envisioned—there, at the very place of temptation and fall, Jesus had to pass through, that he might take up and repair the thread of the interrupted adventure.

Let us not be too hasty to assume that success was a foregone conclusion, that what had been a risk for the first Adam and had become an impossibility for his descendants was after all relatively easy for Jesus, since he was God made man in person. Would not the divine power that inhabited him necessarily have to triumph over the human weakness in him? Was Jesus not assured of success? In the theologian's hindsight, surely. But not for the interior experience of Jesus, cruelly torn between a connivance with sin that was not less than ours—since it had really taken on all the consequences of sin—and a love whose demands he alone could comprehend with the very acuity of God.

We can even suppose in him, precisely because he was both man and God, so perfect and refined a sensibility that, far more than any other human being, Jesus had to suffer this inner rending, of which our own temptations today retain but a faint echo. What repercussions for the humanity of the Son of God, who found himself exhausted by hunger, staggering under the weight of temptation, threatened by despair on the cross, and finally obliged to pass through the failure of death—he, the Lord of life! The bloody sweat, the desperate appeals at Gethsemane, and the loud cries issued from the cross have preserved an echo for us. God himself brushed closely by evil and death—what could be more frightful!

In comparison with the great temptations of Jesus, ours appear almost minor, even if they remain decisive and strictly inevitable. But Jesus has preceded us and blazed a trail. He has experienced the horrors of temptation and abandoned himself to his Father. And he always remains here with us, in every temptation even down to the last, that of our agony and death. None of our temptations will ever be as heavy as those of Jesus, for our fragility is not as great as was his. On the contrary, Jesus has totally used up our fragility. But, above all, from now on every temptation contains within itself the paschal strength of Jesus. There, where sin abounded, grace has abounded all the more (Rom 5:20). There, where we are weak, in Jesus we are strong (2 Cor 12:10).

## Second Sunday of Lent

### Matthew 17:1-9

*Jesus took Peter, James, and his brother John and led them up a high mountain by themselves. And he was transfigured before them; his face became bright as the sun, and his clothes became dazzlingly white. And behold, Moses and Elijah appeared and were conversing with him. Then Peter spoke up and said to Jesus, "Lord, it is good for us to be here! If you wish, I will pitch three tents here, one for you, one for Moses, and one for Elijah." While he was still speaking, a bright cloud came and overshadowed them, and from the cloud came a voice that said, "This is my beloved son, upon whom I have placed all my love. Listen to him!" On hearing this, the disciples were seized with great fear and fell with their faces to the ground. But Jesus approached, touched them, and said, "Rise, and do not fear!" Raising their eyes, they saw no one else but Jesus alone.*

*As they came down the mountain, Jesus gave them this command: "Tell no one the vision you have seen, until the Son of Man has been raised from the dead."*

The event was a total surprise. Jesus' face, like the sun; his clothes, like light; two apparitions, a few scraps of conversation, a voice coming from the cloud. The apostles take fright and fall face down to the ground.

Do they still recognize Jesus? Space and time have expanded. Moses and Elijah, glorious figures of the past, are there conversing familiarly with him, as if they were used to chatting every day like neighbors and contemporaries. Heaven has been opened, as if it had never been closed but continued unceasingly to touch the earth. And the Father has spoken, as if he had always been addressing human beings. Jesus alone is not surprised. In his eyes, all this is very ordinary, his daily fare, the deepest reality of his being—Jesus, himself, temporarily hidden from our gaze.

When the event has passed, when the light and the prophets have disappeared and the Father's voice has fallen silent, the same Jesus will come to touch his disciples with his—once again very ordinary—hand to rouse them from their quasi-comatose panic. "Rise, and do not fear." Daring at last to raise their eyes, they no longer see anyone but him, Jesus alone.

It is once again the everyday Jesus who is familiar to them and who inspires only confidence and love. They are reassured. But do they understand? And are we able to understand? They knew Jesus as they were used to seeing him every day, as one of their own. Then they saw him just now radiating light and glory, almost a different being. And now, once again, they see him as before, the everyday Jesus, one of their own. Still the same Jesus. But who is he, really?

Jesus goes on, moreover, to burden them with a weighty secret. They have seen him as the others never have and would not be able to understand it. To speak of it with them would serve no purpose. "Jesus thus forbade them," says the evangelist; "Tell no one the vision you have seen until the Son of Man has been raised from the dead." This dazzling glory of Jesus, his proximity to the whole of salvation history, represented by Moses and Elijah, his dialogue and his intimacy with the Father, this treasure that he carries hidden within himself, must remain secret for the time being. It cannot be rightly understood except in the light of his Passover, his death and resurrection.

The three apostle-witnesses have perceived only an initial, passing reflection of this mystery, whose import still eludes them. One of the evangelists even remarks that on descending from Mount Tabor, they discussed among themselves what "rising from the dead" might mean. They too, even though they will never forget the event, will not grasp until later the meaning of this premonitory Transfiguration. Just as it was necessary for Jesus to go through his Passover—that is to say, that he should die and rise—in order that his true face of glory and light might be apprehended, the disciples in their turn must also first go through their own Passover, must die and rise with Jesus, before they will know him in glory and then be allowed to pitch their tents and remain with him, in glory, forever.

As long as we are on the way to Easter, the glory of Jesus' face normally remains hidden from us. Our own glory, as well. The marvelous epic of salvation history is most often reduced to the present moment, where we forget the past and dread the future. And we are deaf to the Father's voice, which, nevertheless, resounds unceasingly. Fortunately, in each of our lives, there have been some luminous mornings of Tabor, those all too fleeting moments of grace that we can never forget, that mark us forever but of which we can hardly speak for lack of the right words. For here each one carries his own secret of glory, of light, of infinite joy. A secret that, one day, will give us the strength to take up the journey to Easter.

# Third Sunday of Lent

## John 4:5-24

*Jesus came to a Samaritan town called Sychar, near the territory that Jacob had given to his son Joseph, and where Jacob's well is found. Jesus, fatigued by his journey, sat down there next to the well. It was about noon. A Samaritan woman came to the well to draw water. Jesus said to her, "Give me a drink." (His disciples had gone into the town to buy something to eat.) The Samaritan woman said to him, "How can you, a Jew, ask me, a Samaritan woman, for a drink?" (For, in fact, Jews have nothing in common with Samaritans.) Jesus said to her in reply, "If you knew the gift of God and who is saying to you, 'Give me a drink,' you would have asked him, and he would have given you living water." She said to him, "Sir, you do not even have a bucket, and the well is deep. Where are you going to get this living water? Are you greater than our father Jacob, who gave us this well and drank from it with his sons and his flocks?" Jesus said to her in reply, "Whoever drinks this water will thirst again. But whoever drinks the water I shall give will never thirst. The water that I give will become in them a spring of water welling up to eternal life." The woman said to him, "Sir, give me this water always, that I may not thirst or have to return here anymore to draw water."*

*Jesus said to her, "Go, call your husband and come back." She replied, "I do not have a husband." Jesus answered, "You are right to say, 'I do not have a husband,' for you have had five husbands, and the one you have now is not your husband. What you have said is true." The woman said to him, "Sir, I can see you are a prophet. Our fathers worshiped God on this mountain, but you people say that the place to worship is in Jerusalem." Jesus said to her, "Believe me, woman, the hour is coming when you will worship the Father neither on this mountain nor in Jerusalem. You people worship what you do not know; we worship what we know, for salvation is from the Jews. But the hour is coming, and is now here, when true worshipers will worship the Father in spirit and in truth. For the Father seeks such worshipers. God is spirit, and those who worship him must worship in spirit and in truth."*

Jesus and the Samaritan woman. Two thirsts come face to face in confrontation. Did the Samaritan woman, then, thirst for Jesus? She does not let it show, except perhaps by this amused smile before a Jew who, against all propriety, addresses himself to her, a woman of bad reputation. Does this stranger, then, thirst for her? Certainly, but not in the way insinuated by the treacherous smile of this woman. Jesus thirsts for her with the thirst that he has for all human beings, a thirst that he dissimulates for the moment behind the request, "Give me a drink."

Jesus has just now violated a taboo, and thus scandalized his apostles, because he knows his own thirst better than anyone: for water, in the first instance, but also for this poor woman who so fails to recognize her own thirst. This thirst of the poor one who does not know herself, this it is that produces Jesus' thirst for the Samaritan woman.

To quench these two thirsts, his own and that of the Samaritan woman, there is only one available means: to suggest to her just how thirsty she is, but with another kind of thirst and for another sort of water—living water—whose source Jesus alone knows.

At length, this woman admits that she has indeed been thirsty in her life. She has had five husbands, not counting the man with whom she now lives. She has peddled her thirst and her desire from door to door, from husband to husband, without ever finding satisfaction. And, little by little, devoured by her own desires, and devouring one provisional partner after another, she has finished by remaining alone yet ever more tortured by thirst.

Her countenance betrays the traces of this torment and touches Jesus' heart. He does not brandish the decalogue of Moses. He does not condemn her. He is moved and has compassion. He welcomes the perhaps troubled interest that she takes in him that he might make her aware of a thirst that she does not know. Jesus intrigues her, but she does not recognize him. She has drunk so much, but of a water that never changes anything fundamentally.

"If you knew the gift of God, and who it is who is speaking with you, you would have asked him, and he would have given you living water." Earthly thirsts are inevitable but relatively easy to quench. They remain on the surface of our humanity, simple signs of other thirsts that sleep in our depths. Like the Samaritan woman, we remain ignorant of these thirsts until Jesus comes in person to awaken them. Often, the same encounter suffices to uncover and enliven these thirsts and simultaneously to satisfy them. For he himself is at once our thirst and its appeasement.

In fact, the one who drinks the water that he gives will never thirst again. Here below, our thirsts and their slaking are relentlessly repeated, always begetting a new thirst that begins the same cycle again. The meeting with Jesus, by contrast, has something definitive about it, eternal. He touches our deepest desire, and this desire does not emerge from the encounter unmarked. It henceforth takes root and finds its source in Jesus, because Jesus both welcomes all our desires and exhausts them. Until we thirst no more. Until we have no desire but for him alone, the Savior of the world.

As for the well to draw from, where Jesus is seated and waits for us, it is not far away. It is within us, in the most secret place of the heart: "The water I shall give," says Jesus, "will become within him a spring of water welling up to eternal life." We will doubtless never be without thirst, but neither will we ever again be short of water. Our desires and their satisfaction will meet in the source, in the intimate depths of our heart, in the life of Jesus who abides within us. There, desire and satiety no longer face off, no longer confront each other, as Jesus and the Samaritan woman did at Jacob's well. Henceforward they will coincide: desire fulfilled beyond all telling, love, peace, and joy in the Holy Spirit.

# Fourth Sunday of Lent

## John 9:1-13, 39-41

*As he was leaving the Temple, Jesus saw a man who had been blind from birth. His disciples asked him: "Rabbi, who sinned, this man or his parents, that he should be born blind?" Jesus replied, "Neither he nor his parents sinned. Rather, it is so that the works of God might be revealed through him. We must do the works of the one who sent me while it is day. For night is coming, when no one can work. While I am in the world, I am the light of the world."*

*When he had said this, he spat on the ground and, making clay with the saliva, smeared it on the eyes of the blind man and said to him, "Go, wash in the pool of Siloam" (a name that means "sent"). Thus the blind man went there and washed. And when he came back, he was able to see.*

*His neighbors, and those who had been accustomed to seeing him begging, said therefore, "Isn't this the one who used to sit and beg?" Some said, "It is." But others said, "No, it only looks like him." But he said, "I am he."*

*And they asked him, "Tell us then, how were your eyes opened?" He said in reply, "The man called Jesus made mud and smeared it on my eyes and said to me, 'Go to Siloam and wash.' So I went, and washed, and now I see." They said to him, "Where is he?" And he responded, "I don't know."*

*Therefore, Jesus said, "I came into the world for judgment, that those who do not see might see, and that those who see might become blind." Some Pharisees who were with him heard this and said to him, "Surely, we are not also blind, are we?" Jesus said to them in reply, "If you were blind, you would have no sin. But now you say, 'We see,' so your sin remains."*

In this gospel, Jesus and the Pharisees confront each other with a blind man in between them. The debate centers on blindness and its cure, on sin and forgiveness, and, more specifically, on the connection between blindness—or any other illness—and sin. Why do we get sick?

For the Pharisees, the answer is obvious. If this man was born blind, the only question that they submit to Jesus is that which seeks to learn who is culpable: the parents or the blind man himself.

Without delay, Jesus cuts short this line of questioning: no, for him, no sickness is a punishment for sin: "Neither he nor his parents sinned." If God has permitted this blindness, it is "that the works of God might be revealed through it."

It was precisely to accomplish these "works of God" that Jesus came into the world: works of healing and of salvation. Moreover, Jesus unites deed and word. He puts a bit of mud on the extinguished eyes of the blind man and orders him to go and wash in the pool. And the miracle is realized.

A miracle all the more unexpected as Jesus accomplishes it, as on other occasions, on the Sabbath. His Father is always at work, even and above all on this day that is consecrated to him, and Jesus can only do what he sees his Father doing. He does the work of his Father even, to all appearances, in violation of the Law.

So the miracle becomes highly improbable in the eyes of the Pharisees. Think of it: a miracle that is equivalent to a sacrilege and that, according to their opinion, places Jesus in the ranks of sinners. Jesus is therefore no better than this ostensibly healed blind man. They make this known to the latter: "This man does not come from God, for he does not observe the Sabbath." However, the formerly blind man replies, "How can a sinner perform such signs?" But the Pharisees release a scathing and self-assured response: "We know that this man is a sinner." And not only Jesus but, for all the more reason, the formerly blind man as well: "You were born entirely in sin, and you would teach us!" And they expel him from the synagogue. If Jesus is guilty of sacrilege, the one who has benefited from this sacrilege can only be a blasphemer.

And the latter has still not seen in Jesus more than a prophet. He has not yet been able to see anything more in him. The healing of his exterior eyes was only a first step. He will meet Jesus a second time, but for the opening of the eyes of his heart. "Do you believe in the Son of Man?" Jesus asks him, thus evoking the divine being announced by Daniel and whose name Jesus appropriates to himself to say that he is Messiah and God. "And who is he, sir, that I may believe in him?" "You have seen him, and it is he who is speaking to you." "I do believe, Lord." And he prostrated himself before him.

Behold, the man blind from birth is henceforth totally healed, soul and body. And, confronted with him, the Pharisees are more than ever blind and hardened. Jesus provides the reason for this. If the man born blind has received his sight, it is because he knew he was blind and he dared to ask for healing from Jesus. If the Pharisees remain desperately blind, it is because they are ignorant of their blindness. Herein lies the overwhelming and contradictory judgment spoken by Jesus, where roles are reversed, and for which he came into the world: "That those who do not see might see, and those who do see might become blind."

"Are we also blind, then?" the Pharisees ask him. Jesus' response is as clear as it is surprising: "If you were blind, you would have no sin. But now you claim to see, so your sin remains."

To be blind? Or a sinner? It matters little. Jesus is here to heal us. But to claim to have sight or to be just is to pass Jesus by and to risk that Jesus, in turn, may pass us by as well.

# Fifth Sunday of Lent

## John 11:1-28, 34-47

*A man had fallen sick. This was Lazarus of Bethany, the village of Mary and of her sister Martha. (It was Mary who anointed the Lord's feet with perfume and wiped them with her hair. The sick man, Lazarus, was her brother.)*

*Therefore, the two sisters sent word to Jesus: "Lord, the one whom you love is sick." On learning this, Jesus said, "This sickness is not to end in death, but is for the glory of God, that the Son of God may be glorified." Now Jesus loved Martha and her sister as well as Lazarus. So, when he heard that he was sick, he remained two days where he was. After that, he said to his disciples, "Let us go back to Judea."*

*The disciples said to him, "Rabbi, the Jews were just trying to stone you, and you want to return there?" Jesus answered, "Are there not twelve hours in a day? The one who walks by day does not stumble, for he sees the light of this world. But the one who walks by night stumbles, because the light is not in him." After saying this, he added, "Our friend, Lazarus, has fallen asleep." The disciples said to him, "Lord, if he is asleep, he will be saved." For they thought that Jesus had meant ordinary sleep, whereas he had speaking of death. Therefore, he said plainly, "Lazarus has died, and for your sake I am glad I was not there, so that you may believe. But let us go to him." Thomas, whose name means "Twin," said to the other disciples, "Let us go with him, to die with him."*

*When Jesus arrived, he found that Lazarus had already been in the tomb for four days. As Bethany was near Jerusalem—about a sabbath day's journey—many of the Jews had come to pay their sympathies to Martha and Mary and to grieve with them.*

*When Martha heard that Jesus had arrived, she went out to meet him, while Mary stayed at home. Martha said to Jesus, "Lord, if you had been here, my brother would not have died. But I know that, even now, God will grant you whatever you ask." Jesus said to her, "Your brother will rise." Martha replied, "I know he will rise, in the resurrection on the last day." Jesus said to her, "I am the resurrection and the life. Whoever believes in me, even if he dies, will live. And whoever lives and believes in me will never die. Do you believe this?" She said in reply, "Yes, Lord. I have come to believe that you are the Messiah, the Son of God, the one who is to come into the world."*

*He asked, "Where have you laid him?" They answered, "Sir, come and see." And Jesus wept. The Jews said to one another, "See how he loved him!" But some of them said, "Could not the one who opened the eyes of the blind man have done something so that Lazarus would not die?"*

*Jesus, seized with emotion, arrived at the tomb. It was a cave sealed with a stone. Jesus said, "Roll back to the stone." Martha, the dead man's sister, said to him, "Lord, by now there will be a stench. He has been dead for four days." Then Jesus said to Martha, "Did I not tell you that, if you believe, you will see the glory of God?" Then they rolled back the stone. And Jesus raised his eyes to heaven and said, "Father, I thank you that you have heard me. I know that you always hear me, but I have said this for the sake of the crowd, that they may believe that you sent me." Then, he cried out in a loud voice, "Lazarus, come out!" And the dead man came out, his hands and feet tied in burial bands and his head covered with a cloth. Jesus said to them, "Untie him and let him go."*

*Many of the Jews who had come to Mary and Martha therefore saw what Jesus did and began to believe in him.*

"This illness will not end in death, but is for the glory of God, that the Son of God may be glorified by it." With these words, Jesus welcomes the news of the (doubtless severe) illness of his friend, Lazarus. Jesus loved Lazarus and his two sisters, Martha and Mary, and he has chosen this illness as the vehicle for a sign that involves Jesus himself and, through his friend, all of us.

This sign required a dead man who was truly dead and not just seemingly dead. The evangelist underlines this fact with several details. First, Jesus waits two days for the confirmation of the death. Then, he still takes his time, surely by design, before setting out on the journey, provoking the sorrowful reproach of the two sisters: "Lord, if you had been here, my brother would not have died." When he arrives, Lazarus has already been buried for four days. The way things stand, people are hesitant to remove the stone from the entrance of the tomb. Surely the corpse will already stink.

Jesus has already given to his disciples a preliminary interpretation of this death: "Our friend Lazarus has fallen asleep." It will suffice to wake him from his slumber. Now, before Lazarus's two sisters, Jesus says something more: Lazarus is dead, of course, but no matter! "Your brother will rise," he says to Martha. Indeed, many of the Jews of that era believed that the dead would rise on the Last Day, and

Martha was no exception. But Jesus clarifies his point: what he has just evoked goes far beyond what she imagines. There is no need to wait for the Last Day. The resurrection stands even now before Martha, he himself: "I am the Resurrection and the Life." A resurrection that is effective even as of now, for Jesus adds, "Whoever believes in me, even if he dies, will live. And whoever lives and believes in me will never die. Do you believe this?"

Even if he dies, he will live, and he who lives will never die. The extraordinary power of faith in Jesus! It renders every death here below merely apparent—in the strict sense of the word—and transforms even terminal illness from a path to death into an occasion for giving glory to God and glorifying his Son.

The resurrection of Lazarus that now follows this declaration of Jesus is but its illustration. Even if it makes the two sisters abound with joy, even if it impresses the people, even if it disturbs the authorities and thus engenders the plot that will issue in Jesus' own death, all this is less important than the very words that Jesus has just pronounced with such solemnity. It is his own death and resurrection that Jesus has just announced as well as our death to ourselves, of which mystery he has just unveiled a small part.

For no one can definitively escape death unless they go by way of Jesus, as the latter has just suggested, that they may finally arrive—also through him—at the resurrection. No one escapes it, not even Lazarus, whose resurrection here is still only provisional, like the others that Jesus performed during his life on earth: the daughter of Jairus, the son of the widow of Nain. Everyone remains destined for the death of the flesh that they may be able to benefit from the resurrection that is Jesus himself.

Despite the miracle that Jesus has just performed on his behalf, Lazarus is hardly privileged with respect to us. At most, he can verify even in his own flesh the power contained in Jesus' words, but in flesh that remains what it was before, not yet the spiritual body that Jesus will clothe with immortality at the resurrection. At least, thanks to Lazarus, we can realize that the sickness and death that await us are but for the glory of God, that our death is but a falling asleep in the mystery of Jesus, and that believing in Jesus is sufficient for eternal life that begins even now.

# Palm Sunday

## Matthew 21:1-11; 27:32-50

*A few days before the feast of Passover, Jesus and his disciples drew near to Jerusalem, arriving at Bethphage on the slope of the Mount of Olives. Jesus sent two of his disciples, saying, "Go into the village opposite you, and you will find an ass tethered along with its colt. Untie them and bring them to me. And if anyone asks what you are doing, say to them, 'The master has need of them and will send them back at once.'" This took place to fulfill the word spoken through the prophet: "Say to Daughter Zion: Behold, your king comes to you, meek and riding on an ass and on a colt, the foal of a beast of burden." The disciples left and did as Jesus had commanded them. They brought the ass and its foal, placed their cloaks over them, and helped Jesus to mount. In the crowd, many spread their cloaks on the path; others cut branches from the trees and strewed them along the road. Those who walked ahead of Jesus as well as those who followed behind cried out, shouting, "Hosanna to the son of David! Blessed is he who comes in the name of the Lord! Hosanna in the highest!" When Jesus entered Jerusalem, the whole city was shaken, asking, "Who is this?" And the crowds responded, "This is Jesus the prophet, from Nazareth in Galilee." . . . As they went out, they found a man named Simon, a Cyrenean, whom they pressed into service to carry the cross. When they came to the place called Golgotha, which is translated "Place of the Skull," they offered Jesus wine mixed with gall, which he tasted but would not drink. After they had crucified him, they divided his garments by drawing lots for them; then they sat there, keeping watch over him. Above him was an inscription naming the cause of his condemnation: "This is Jesus, the king of the Jews." At the same time, two bandits were crucified with him, one on his right and the other on his left. Those passing by shook their heads at him: "You, who would destroy the Temple and rebuild it in three days, save yourself—if you are the Son of God—and come down from the cross!" The chief priests, together with the scribes and the elders, likewise mocked him and said, "He saved others, he cannot save himself! Let the king of Israel come down from the cross now, that we may see and believe in him! He trusted in God, let him deliver him now, if he wants him. For he said, 'I am the Son of God.'" The criminals crucified with him also kept insulting him in the same way.*

*Darkness then came over the whole earth from noon until three in the afternoon. Around three o'clock, Jesus cried out in a loud voice, "Eli, Eli, lema sabachthani?" which means, "My God, my God! Why have you abandoned me?"*

*On hearing him, some of the bystanders said, "Listen, he is calling the prophet Elijah!" At once, one of them ran and picked up a sponge, which he soaked in a vessel of vinegar; he placed it on the tip of a reed and gave it to Jesus to drink. But the others said, "Wait! Let us see if Elijah comes to save him." But Jesus again raised a loud cry and gave up his spirit.*

Jesus meets his Passover in a state of utter distress. Taking along three of his disciples, he "began to feel anguish and distress," the evangelist tells us. "My soul could die of sorrow!" says Jesus. His sadness is like a foretaste of death itself. One could scarcely imagine Jesus more broken and tormented than one finds him at Gethsemane.

His disciples fare no better. Indeed, in a certain sense, they do much worse. Invited by Jesus to keep company with him in his prayer, not grasping the gravity of the moment, they three times yield to sleep. When the soldiers finally appear, they abandon Jesus and take flight.

We have not yet mentioned Peter, who just now bravely pledged his loyalty to Jesus: "Even if all fall away from you, yet I will never fall away" (Matt 26:33). Despite a clumsy attempt at striking with the sword and an initial following of Jesus affected from afar, Peter will be the first to fall, in the face of a servant girl's insinuations.

The passion is thus inaugurated with fear, a general fear. That of Jesus, but also that of his apostles, of the chief priests, who fear reprisals from the Roman occupiers, and finally of the Roman governor himself, who wants to avoid public disorder and to retain the emperor's favor. Each one in turn succumbs to his own fear—with the exception of Jesus.

Not that he did not experience the fear gripping his entrails. But he did not run away from his fear, accepting the need to pass through it instead. Not the way we would like to have passed through it: confronting it courageously, showing off before it, claiming to triumph over it. Rather, he did it the way that we, being such as we are, would surely have done it: in humility, in weakness, letting himself be torn, worked over, quartered by it. Another evangelist will evoke the bloody sweat (Luke 22:44), and the author of the Epistle to the Hebrews will recall his cries and tears (Heb 5:7). Jesus did not flee the trial by fear. He simply agreed to pass through it.

How did he do it? He himself has confided to us the secret in the form of a counsel for whenever we find ourselves invited to enter, in our turn, into the same drama, the drama of our own passion: "Watch and pray, that you may not fall at the hour of temptation!" Outside of prayer, there can be no other outcome but that of succumbing to fear and taking flight. The reason is simple, and it holds true both for Jesus and for us: only the spirit is ardent, while the flesh is so incorrigibly weak. For Jesus too, because the difficulty of his combat consisted precisely in this assumed flesh that is ours as well, still wounded by our sin, and that only a resurrection after death could heal.

Jesus expressed this ardor of the spirit—already now stronger than the weakness of the flesh—in a prayer formula of which the apostles retained some fragments. First: "My Father, if it is possible, let this cup pass from me!" Jesus does not play the hero. He does not conceal his fear. Rather, he confirms it but presents it before his Father. He thereby makes it the material of his prayer. His Father will understand all the weight of his fear.

Then: "Yet not what I desire, but what you desire." Jesus' initial desire is that of his flesh, of our flesh. He is afraid and wants to avoid what threatens him. But fear is not a desire. It is only terror experienced in the face of desire, or before another's desire. It ties up, it blocks the way; it never liberates. There is only one way to turn fear away. Jesus offers it to his Father's desire, that is, to his love. "Not this fear that would induce me to flee, Father, but what you, in your love, desire for me." For all our fears are fears of love. And only love, true love, can heal them.

# Holy Thursday

## John 13:1-15

*Before the feast of Passover, Jesus, knowing that the hour had come for him to pass from this world to the Father, and having always loved his own in the world, loved them to the end. While they were at table, when the devil had already induced Judas, son of Simon the Iscariot, to betray him, Jesus—knowing that the Father had handed all things over to him, and that he had come from God and was going back to God—rose from the table, took off his outer garment, and put a towel around his waist. Then he poured water in a basin and began to wash his disciples' feet and to dry them with the towel around his waist. When he came to Simon Peter, Peter said to him, "Lord, are you going to wash my feet?" Jesus said to him, "What I want to do, you do not understand now, but you will understand later." Peter said to him, "You will never wash my feet!" Jesus said in reply, "Unless I wash you, you will have no part with me." Simon Peter said to him, "Then not only my feet, Lord, but my hands and head as well." Jesus said to him, "One who has bathed has no need except to have feet washed, for he is clean all over. So, you are clean . . . but not all." For he himself knew who was going to betray him; for this reason, he said, "Not all of you are clean."*

*When he had finished washing their feet, he put his garment back on and took his place at the table. Then he said to them, "Do you understand what I have done for you? You call me 'Master' and 'Lord,' and rightly so, for so I am. If I, therefore, the Lord and Master, have washed your feet, you also ought to wash each other's feet. I have given you an example to follow, so that as I have done for you, you should also do."*

He loved them to the end. Of this "love to the end," Jesus has bequeathed to us two memorials. First: "Do this in memory of me." Bread and wine, signs of his body handed over and of his blood poured out. Then: "I have given you an example to follow, that you in turn must wash one another's feet": a sign of humble service. Both of these, the Eucharist and the foot washing, are memorial and sacrament of love to the end, for there is no greater love than to give one's life for those whom one loves.

Even today, to keep the memorial of Jesus is to repeat unceasingly these two signs, that of love unto death, and that of the love that humbles itself in service of the brothers and sisters. For these two sacraments complement one another: self-effacement in death, self-effacement in service.

To celebrate the memorial of Jesus, however, is much more than piously to remember the past. The paschal memorial is, we could say, an extendable memorial. It not only commemorates the past, but it brings the past into the present. The memory of Jesus' past becomes the burning actuality of the church and of the world today. Jesus is present at the heart of the community that reenacts the Last Supper. He is also present among those who humbly serve their brothers and sisters. It is impossible to resemble him more closely than that: "I have given you an example to follow that, as I have done for you, you must also do." Impossible more efficaciously to reveal Jesus to the world: "By this all will know that you are my disciples, if you have love for one another" (John 13:35).

There is more. Not only does this memory bring the past into our today, but it also projects it into the future. It is a memory that anticipates, a memory that, being already a certitude today, is also hope for tomorrow. At the hour of the Last Supper, at the moment when he shared the cup, Jesus is conscious of this: "From now on," he says, "I will not drink this cup until I drink it anew in my Father's kingdom" (Matt 26:29). For him, past, present, and future already touch one another and are almost confounded. It is essential to Jesus' Passover that it is a crucial moment at the center of history, a uniquely dense convergence point that in a sense will never be recovered, but that at the same time will remain forever available and can for that reason be unceasingly repeated. The Passover of Jesus encompasses at once the past, the present, and the coming eternity.

Saint Paul was also aware of this when he sometimes spoke to us about the Eucharist: "Whenever you eat this bread and drink this cup, you proclaim the death of the Lord until he comes." Past, present, and future are juxtaposed and telescoped, as likewise when we sing during the eucharistic prayer in response to the narration of the Supper, "We proclaim your death, O Lord, and confess your resurrection, until you come again."

The humble love of the brother or sister, expressed in the sacrament of the foot washing, is no less marked by the same density, the same prolongation into history. It too encompasses the totality of the mystery. It reproduces among us the example left by Jesus. It renders Jesus present in the persons of all those who have received the gift of serving in self-effacement. And it propels them already, so to speak, beyond their death into the coming kingdom. As the apostle John was able to say so eloquently, "If Jesus laid down his life for us, we too ought to lay down our lives for our brothers and sisters. And we know that we have already passed from death to life, because we love the brothers and sisters" (John 3:14).

It is in this way that we have celebrated this evening the memorial of Jesus, entering in our turn into his liturgical Passover, at the heart of salvation history. "For just as he was, so too are we in this world" (1 John 4:17).

# Good Friday

## John 18:28-40

*Then they brought Jesus from Caiphas to the praetorium. It was morning. The Jews did not enter the praetorium themselves, lest they defile themselves and become unable to eat the Passover. Pilate therefore came outside to speak with them: "What charge do you bring against this man?" They responded, "If he were not a criminal, we would not have handed him over to you." Pilate said to them, "Take him and judge him yourselves according to your own law." The Jews responded, "We are not allowed to put a man to death." This was to fulfill the word that Jesus had spoken to indicate the kind of death he was going to die. Then Pilate went back into the praetorium, summoned Jesus, and said to him, "Are you the king of the Jews?" Jesus asked him, "Do you ask me this of your own accord or because others have told you about me?" Pilate responded, "Am I a Jew? It is your own nation and the chief priests who have handed you over to me: what have you done?" Jesus answered, "My kingdom is not of this world; if my kingdom were of this world, my retainers would have fought to prevent me from being handed over to the Jews, but my kingdom is not of this kind." Pilate then said to him, "Then, you are a king?" Jesus replied, "It is you who say I am a king. For this I was born, and for this I came into the world, to testify to the truth.*

*Whoever belongs to the truth listens to my voice." Pilate said to him, "What is truth?" After this, he went out again to the Jews, and he said to them, "I have found in this man no grounds for condemnation. But you have the custom that I should release to you one prisoner at Passover time: shall I release to you the king of the Jews?" But they all began to cry out, "Not this man! Release to us Barabbas!" (Now Barabbas was a bandit.)*

*Then Pilate commanded that Jesus be taken off to be flogged. The soldiers fashioned a crown of thorns and placed it on his head, and they clothed him in a purple cloak. Then they approached him and cried out, saying, "Hail, King of the Jews!" And they spat upon him.*

*Pilate went out again and spoke to the Jews: "Behold, I will bring him out to you so that you may know that I find no case against him." Then Jesus came out, wearing the crown of thorns and the purple cloak. And Pilate said to them, "Behold, the man!" When they saw him, the chief priests and the guards began to cry out, "Crucify him! Crucify him!" Pilate said to them, "Take him yourselves and crucify him, for I find no case against him!" The Jews responded, "We have a law, and according to this law he must die, because he made himself the Son of God." When Pilate heard these words, he was more afraid than ever. He went back into the praetorium and said to Jesus, "Where do you come from?" But Jesus gave him no answer. Pilate said to him, therefore, "Do you refuse to speak to me? Do you not know that I have power to release you and power to crucify you?" Jesus said in reply, "You would have no power over me if it had not been given you from above; therefore, the one who handed me over to you has the greater sin." From that moment, Pilate sought to release him. But the Jews began to cry out, "If you release him, you are not a friend of Caesar. Everyone who makes himself king opposes Caesar." When he heard this, Pilate brought Jesus outside and had him sit at the judge's bench at a place called Stone Pavement, in Hebrew Gabbatha. It was a Friday, the day before Passover, around noon. Pilate said to the Jews, "Behold your king." Then they shouted, "Away with him! Away with him! Crucify him!" Pilate said to them, "Shall I crucify your king?" The chief priests responded, "We have no king but Caesar." Then, he handed him over to them to be crucified, and they seized him.*

"They crucified him," a laconic and atrocious expression, an unbearable spectacle. And yet, the physical suffering endured by Jesus can surely not be compared to his interior suffering: a sense of total failure. On the previous Sunday morning, the crowd had acclaimed him: "Blessed is he who comes in the name of the Lord! Blessed be the king of Israel!" The following Friday, his royalty is turned to derision by all. He will finally be the only one to affirm it again, joined only by Pilate, who, without knowing what he is doing, will insist on keeping this inscription above the cross, "Jesus of Nazareth, king of the Jews," with the sole purpose of exasperating the Jews.

At present, all are mocking his kingship. The soldiers, first of all, at the scene of the crowning of thorns, so trying and humiliating for him who truly knew himself to be king. Then the Jewish crowds, stirred up against him by the Pharisees, who are bent on his death as they see him appear, no longer in the paraphernalia of a king but rather of a clown. And then there is the governor himself, who, cynical and perfidious, makes use of Jesus' kingship to humiliate the Jews' national pride by condemning to death their supposed king, and that at their own request. Jesus the king is no more than a masquerade king, the victim of a cruel and base political game, a king whom mutual antagonists exploit to each other's disadvantage.

This initial failure of Jesus is coupled with another, much crueler still. Leaving aside the fact that his own people have treated him thus . . . what about his Father? The Messiah, the one sent by God, can he also fail so lamentably? That was unthinkable for the priests and the elders. This agony on the cross is in their eyes the hitherto missing proof that Jesus was merely an impostor: "So, this is the king of Israel: let him come down from the cross now and we will believe in him." More venomous, and more painful to the heart of the Father's beloved Son, are the words they add: "He trusted in God; let God deliver him now if he loves him!" "If he loves him!" Even the Father's love, with which Jesus had found himself continually surrounded, is now cast into doubt and seems to be withheld.

Nothing worse could happen to him. If he has to doubt his own people, so be it. But must he doubt even his Father as well? And nothing could be more upsetting to him than that his own people, in the person of the leaders, should instill in his heart such a frightful doubt. The fiasco could not be more lacerating or more inexorable. "My God, my God, why have you forsaken me?"

If Jesus had ceded to such a doubt, that would have constituted the lamentable and definitive end of the whole of salvation history. Thus a second catastrophe would have succeeded the first, that of Adam in the terrestrial paradise, and would have forever confirmed it. That could have happened, and in a certain sense it would even have been humanly foreseeable. Jesus' disaster would then have been merely the logical consequence of Adam's primordial fall. With a body wounded by sin, as is every body that has come into the world since Adam, how was Jesus able to fare better than we do? How was Jesus able to turn what seemed a fiasco into a way to salvation, a masterpiece of redemption and of healing?

The answer is simple: "Offering loud cries and tears," explains the author of the Epistle to the Hebrews, "Jesus was heard because of the love that was his as Son" (Heb 5:7). But such a certainty of being loved cannot be had by any human being since the fall of Adam. Only Jesus could know such a love: a confident, filial love that passes through and dissipates the doubt has transformed death into a path of life for Jesus, and for us in his wake. For the echo of those words from Jesus' lips that Scripture has preserved for us can become our own prayer today, on the threshold of every great trial and until the hour of our death: "Father, into your hands I commend my spirit."

## Easter Sunday

Matthew 28:1-10

*After the sabbath, very early on the first day of the week, Mary Magdalene and the other Mary came to see the tomb of Jesus. And behold, there was a great earthquake. The angel of the Lord descended from heaven, rolled back the stone, and sat upon it. His appearance was like lightning, and his clothes were white as snow. The guards were seized with fear of him and became like dead men. But the angel addressed the women and said, "Do not be afraid! I know that you seek Jesus, the Crucified. He is not here, for he has been raised as he said. Come, behold the place where he lay. But go and tell his disciples: he has been raised from the dead and he goes before you to Galilee; there you will see him. Behold, I have told you." They left the tomb in haste, fearful yet overjoyed, and ran to announce the news to the disciples. And behold, Jesus met them on their way and said to them, "Peace be with you." They approached him, grasped his feet, and did him homage. Then Jesus said to them, "Do not be afraid. But go and tell my brothers to go to Galilee. There they will see me."*

The Sabbath that preceded the Passover was different from the others. It is scarcely over when the holy women make haste to the tomb. They suppose that it is all that remains to them of Jesus: a tomb, the sole meeting place with Jesus crucified and asleep in death.

But this Passover had not been like the others, like all those that had succeeded one another down the centuries, since the crossing of the Red Sea. So many lambs, "without blemish, male, and a year old," had been immolated on this holy night, before being consumed by believers with staff in hand, in reenacting the exodus of old. But this time the Paschal Lamb had been of a different sort. It was the absolutely unique lamb to which all the preceding ones had pointed: the Lamb of God, come to take away the sins of the world (John 1:29).

As they hurried to the tomb, the holy women were prepared to identify a corpse. What awaited them was completely different. They expected to find Jesus at repose in the tomb. Yet he is no longer there; his repose there is over with, the angel assures them. They have only to look to verify it: "Come and see the place where he lay." Then, finally, the surprising good news: "He has been raised, just as he said."

Did they at once believe the angel's words? A mix of fear and of joy restrains them. "Fearful yet overjoyed," they run off to bear the good news to the disciples. But they do so in vain, according to another evangelist, for the men refuse to lend credence to these "women's tales" (Mark 16:11).

But they? Of course, when they run out from the tomb, they still know only by hearsay, by the angel's testimony, even if their feminine intuition and the feeling in their hearts preceded all other evidence. But they could neither see nor touch Jesus. There is not even any evident astonishment on their part. "He is not here," the angel told them truly.

"He is not here?" And yet, scarcely had they begun their mission to the disciples when, on a detour from the path, Jesus appears to them in the radiant light of that Sunday dawn. He was therefore there, after all! He lets himself be seen this time, even touched, in his risen flesh and bones. Henceforth they know him beyond mere hearsay. Their eyes have seen, their hands have touched. Never again will they doubt that Jesus is truly alive.

It is the mystery of the paschal presence of Jesus that extends even until today in our faith and in the faith of the church. The pre-Easter Jesus, living or dead according to the flesh, is no longer here. In vain would we desire to restore him to his former state. Nevertheless, he is more than ever here, according to the Spirit, risen and forever living. He even promised to remain with us all days, until the end of the world (Matt 28:20). But he makes himself visible and palpable only to our faith, to the eyes and hands of believers.

The formulas of the Creed or of the catechism are not sufficient of themselves. They generally permit only knowledge on the level of hearsay unless they become suddenly the privileged instrument of the encounter. But that depends neither on us nor on the catechist nor even on the church, but only and gratuitously on him, Jesus risen. One morning, or one evening, or perhaps preferably by night, on a detour from the path, or in the silence of one's private room, as he wills and when he wills. It is enough for us to desire it, to ask for it, and to consent to wait for it.

When the hour has come for any one of us, we will meet him, like the holy women, with two indications that never fail: a holy and sweet fear—which is the opposite of dread—and an unspeakable joy, two unmistakable signs of love. And we will no more be able to doubt than they were: yes, he is truly risen. And we will make haste, irresistibly impelled to announce it everywhere, as "fearful yet overjoyed" as they were.

# Second Sunday of Easter

## John 20:19-31

*On the first day of the week, when the disciples were gathered together behind locked doors, for fear of the Jews, Jesus came and stood in their midst and said, "Peace be with you." And as he said this, he showed them his hands and his side. The disciples rejoiced when they saw the Lord. Jesus said to them again: "Peace be with you. As the Father sent me, so I send you." When he had said this, he breathed on them and said, "Receive the Holy Spirit. Whose sins you forgive are forgiven them; whose sins you retain are retained."*

*Now Thomas, called Didymus, one of the Twelve, was not with them when Jesus came. Therefore, the others said to him, "We have seen the Lord!" But he said to them, "Unless I see the nail marks in his hands, and put my finger into the nail marks, and put my hand into his side, I will not believe!"*

*Eight days later, the disciples were again in the house, and Thomas was with them. Jesus came, and although the doors were locked, he entered and stood in their midst. He said to them, "Peace be with you." Then he said to Thomas, "Bring your finger here and see my hands. Bring your hand and put it into my side. And doubt no longer, but believe." Thomas answered and said to him, "My Lord and my God." Jesus said to him, "You believe because you have seen me. Blessed are those who have not seen yet believe."*

*Now Jesus performed many other signs in the presence of his disciples that are not written in this book. But these are written so that you may believe that Jesus is the Messiah, the Son of God, and that through your faith you may have life in his name.*

Within the early Christian community in Jerusalem, there were those who had seen the risen Jesus with their own eyes and those who had not. The first were designated as eyewitnesses of the resurrection: his apostles and certain disciples, the holy women, no doubt the Virgin Mary as well. They were well known within the community. Paul recalls that "some are still living, while others have fallen asleep" (1 Cor 15:6).

These eyewitnesses were absolutely necessary to the primitive church for the solid foundation of her faith. Without their testimony, no one could have known of the resurrection. That is so, even if they were not always taken at their word, as Thomas's incredulity reminds us. Nor had they themselves always recognized Jesus at first. Usually it was only with a second look that their eyes were opened, the eyes of their hearts rather than their bodily eyes.

No doubt they were accorded a certain veneration on the part of those who had not seen, and perhaps they were the object of the latters' envy as well. There were those favored with a vision of the Risen One, and then there were the rest. Early on, the question must have been raised as to which of the two camps had received the better portion and constituted the truly privileged.

It is in such a context that John remembers the word spoken by Jesus in the scene with Thomas, who had demanded to see before consenting to believe: "You believe because you have seen me. Blessed are those who have not seen and yet believe." The eyewitnesses are in no way privileged. It is not the corporeal vision of the Risen One that matters, but the vision of faith: those who believe without having seen, or, according to the variant employed by Peter in his epistle, congratulating his correspondents because "without having seen him, you love him" (1 Pet 1:8).

Twenty centuries later, our situation is a bit different. Now the whole church is obliged to walk by faith. We can only believe by relying on the testimony of the eyewitnesses. For all that, our situation is not inferior to theirs. Did they glory in having known Christ according to the flesh? That matters little, Paul would tell them: "Even if we once knew Christ according to the flesh, now we know him thus no longer" (2 Cor 5:16). We know him according to the Spirit, that is, according to the eyes of our faith—the same faith, basically, that was required for Peter, John, Mary Magdalene, and the disciples at Emmaus to be able finally to recognize Jesus Risen in the appearance that presented itself to them. The same faith that Thomas needed in order that the marks of the glorious wounds of the Risen One would allow him to identify the Crucified.

"One cannot see truly except with the eyes of the heart." This celebrated saying clearly applies to our faith in the Risen One. But because our hearts are not all in an identical state, and because each of our hearts changes through the different stages of our spiritual growth, the vision of the Risen One will necessarily differ from one believer to another and even from one moment to the next. It can become increasingly luminous, but it can also become increasingly obscure and even end up disappearing from our horizon.

Though we know and love Jesus now, more or less, we are called always to love him more. However, that will depend on the condition of our hearts' changing in one manner or another. For the two pilgrims to Emmaus, it required that their hearts be set on fire so that they might be able to recognize Jesus (Luke 24:32). It is the same for us. We already know Jesus a little. But we have to ask Jesus unceasingly to increase our faith, so that we might always be able to see him more clearly and love him more intensely.

That is why we are at no disadvantage with respect to the eyewitnesses of the resurrection. The gift that they received was not meant for themselves alone but chiefly for us and for the church. And, as with us, it was not with their bodily eyes that they recognized Jesus Risen, but with the eyes of their hearts: far more "blessed," in fact, "are those who have not seen and yet believe."

# Third Sunday of Easter

## Luke 24:13-35

*On the third day after Jesus' death, two of the disciples were making their way to a village called Emmaus, about seven miles from Jerusalem, and were conversing together about all these things that had taken place. And it happened that while they were thus conversing and debating, Jesus himself drew near and walked with them, but their eyes were prevented from recognizing him. Jesus said to them, "What are you discussing as you walk along the way?" They stopped, looking downcast. One of them, named Cleopas, said in reply, "Are you the only visitor to Jerusalem who does not know of the things that have taken place there in these days?" He said to them, "What sort of things?" They answered, "The things that happened to Jesus of Nazareth, who was a prophet mighty in deed and word before God and all the people, how the chief priests and our rulers both handed him over to a sentence of death and crucified him. But we had hoped that he would be the one to redeem Israel! Moreover, it is now three days since this took place. But some women from our number have astonished us! They went to the tomb early this morning and did not find his body, but rather they came to us saying that they had a vision of angels who announced that he was alive. Some of our companions went to the tomb and found things exactly as the women had said, but him they did not see."*

*Then he said to them, "Oh, how foolish you are, and how slow of heart to believe all that the prophets said! Was it not necessary that the Messiah should suffer and so enter his glory?" Then, beginning from Moses and all the prophets, he interpreted for them what pertained to him in all the Scripture. As they approached the village to which they were headed, Jesus made as if he were going on farther. But they pressed him: "Stay with us, for the evening draws near and the day is already ending!" So he went in and stayed with them.*

*While he was reclining at table with them, he took bread, said the blessing, broke it, and gave it to them. With that, their eyes were opened and they recognized him, but he immediately vanished from their sight. Then they said to one another, "Were not our hearts burning within us as he spoke to us on the way and opened the Scriptures to us?"*

*At that very hour, they got up and returned to Jerusalem, where they found the eleven apostles and those with them who were saying, "The Lord has truly been raised and has appeared to Simon!" Then the two recounted what had taken place on the way and how he had been made known to them in the breaking of the bread.*

The two disciples of Emmaus walk two long hours without recognizing their traveling companion. Jesus was there, at their side, and they did not recognize him. He spoke to them, and they did not understand him. And the great irony: it is to him that they complain about a certain Jesus who had just been taken from them in death; it is before him that they enumerate all their grounds for being sad at his absence, while their happiness is right there at their elbow, within reach. Could Jesus be any closer? He was their companion on the journey, and they didn't know it.

But this lasted only for a time, not definitively; till the end of the day's journey, not till the end of their life. This end of the road can be more or less long. It can sometimes seem to last a long time, to put to the test our faith in Jesus and our love for him that would wish him more immediately tangible. But this end of the road is not destined to be forever prolonged or to terminate in a cul-de-sac. One day, we will arrive. Jesus will make himself known there where we had never imagined him, there where we had never dared to believe in him, there where we were sometimes close to despair—but where he was already present, invisibly present, as for the two disciples of Emmaus.

Our way will not be so different from theirs. First, because Jesus risen is already really with us, as he was with them, and it matters little if we don't yet see him. Strictly speaking, we don't have to reach Jesus; he has forestalled us. We don't have to catch up with him; he has already joined us. We don't have to search for him; he has been given to us beforehand. And this presence, even if it is still obscure, silent, hidden, is what gives our life all its density today; this presence of Jesus at our side is our secret yet most profound joy of living.

Little by little, as we persevere along the way, Jesus will take shape before us, he will reveal himself to the eyes of our heart. First, and above all, in the words of the gospels and of the Bible, "Jesus interpreted for them," as we have heard, "what pertained to him in all the Scripture." For us too, it will happen that a word of Scripture suddenly explodes and catches fire. How many times we had read it, heard it, proclaimed it, even preached and commented on it, yet never until now had it been revealed to us to what an extent each scriptural word is pregnant in the strongest sense of the term: Jesus risen.

Jesus will also take the form of the pilgrims and the poor whom we welcome along our paths. What an unlooked-for opportunity for the two disciples of Emmaus, to have dared to invite home their mysterious companion and to offer him food and shelter for the night! "Stay with us, for evening draws near and the day is already ending!" So many men and women cross our paths, and there is not one among them who has not been created and modeled "in the image of Jesus," not one who would not be capable of touching us with some reflection of his beauty.

Finally, Jesus will reveal himself to us in the breaking of the bread that, even today, after two thousand years, reunites all Jesus' disciples around the same act of communion and of extraordinary presence. In fact, whoever may be the minister who once again performs this action that has become so familiar to us, in memory of Jesus, it is Jesus in person who repeats it at the heart of his church.

To read and listen to the Word, to welcome the brother or sister, to break and eat the eucharistic bread: three ways by which Jesus comes to meet us and to reveal himself to our gaze. Three ways that presuppose something else besides. For to recognize Jesus it will not suffice to know the Scriptures, nor to devote oneself body and soul to others, nor to repeat mechanically the actions of the Last Supper, if warmth of love is still lacking. Without at least a little love for Jesus, it is impossible to perceive him beside us: "Were not our hearts burning within us," confess the two disciples, "as he spoke to us on the way?" Only love is discerning, only love knows. Not that love to which we try somehow to apply ourselves in our best moments, but that which God himself pours unceasingly into our hearts, by the Holy Spirit who has been given to us (Rom 5:5); this divine love will end up making us lean and fall down, irresistibly and yet freely, at Jesus' side.

# Fourth Sunday of Easter

## John 10:1-10

*Jesus said to the Pharisees, "Amen, amen, I say to you, whoever does not enter the sheepfold through the gate, but climbs over elsewhere, is a thief and a robber. The one who enters through the gate is the shepherd of the sheep. The gatekeeper opens to him, and the sheep hear his voice as he calls them by name and leads them out. When he has led out all his sheep, he goes ahead of them, and they follow him because they recognize his voice. They will not follow a stranger, but they will flee from him, because they do not recognize the voice of strangers." Although Jesus used this parable in speaking to the Pharisees, they did not understand his meaning. So, again, Jesus said, "Amen, amen, I say to you, I am the gate for the sheep. All those who came before me were thieves and robbers, but the sheep did not listen to them. I am the gate. If anyone enters through me, he will be saved. He will come in and go out and find pasture. The thief comes only to steal and plunder and destroy. I came so that they might have life and have it abundantly."*

"They recognize his voice and they follow him." In this way, Jesus describes the relationship between the sheep and their shepherd, between himself and his disciples. A mysterious intimacy, a sacred complicity. They don't recognize the voice of strangers, and they don't follow them.

From where, then, do the sheep derive this exact knowledge of Jesus' voice? Before they were in a position to recognize Jesus, they had already been recognized by him; before they were capable of identifying him, they had been identified by him: "The shepherd," says Jesus, "calls each one by name, since they are his own."

Jesus calls them by name. Ever since he became man, and especially since his wounds and his death have healed us, we belong to him by a new and very particular title. As Saint Peter reminds us in the second reading, we had formerly all gone astray like sheep, but now we have returned to him, to the shepherd who watches over us.

The name that Jesus gives us is new, and each of us, as Revelation foretells, will alone have knowledge of it (Rev 2:17). It will remain an eternal secret between Jesus and us. For it is the name of love, what we are to him and what he is to us. Our absolutely unique vocation. A name that seals the love and the intimacy that unite us to him.

One day, Jesus pronounced it into the ears of our heart, in absolute secrecy, perhaps in a moment of silence and prayer, or in the midst of distress and temptation, or at a moment when a word of the Gospel suddenly appeared to shine before our eyes. There was the name, but, still more important, there was the tone with which it was pronounced, the grave warmth of his voice, the weight of love that it communicated—hence from now on our new name and Jesus' voice coincide. Impossible to recognize the one without the other. Impossible to discern who we are for him without knowing ourselves ardently loved by him.

How then, can we henceforth fail to recognize the voice of Jesus among the thousand other voices that assail us and summon us? His voice is unique, for it belongs at once to himself and to me. And how can we not have a blind confidence in it, since recognizing the voice of Jesus is at the same time being confirmed in the joy that I feel at being so greatly loved by him.

And how can we hesitate even an instant to respond to his call? If he calls me, it is for me to rise and follow him. "When he leads out all his sheep," Jesus continues, "he goes ahead of them, and they follow him." Where, therefore? Wherever Jesus will go. The way along which he travels matters little, since henceforth he himself is the one and only Way that he has personally opened for us, that he might become for us the head of the new humanity, born on Easter night. While we are with him, how could we be going the wrong way?

And the gate, that too is he. Jesus has just insisted upon it in the Gospel: "I am the gate for the sheep. . . . If anyone enters by me, he will be saved. He will come in, and go out, and find pasture." If we try obstinately, with the gentle obstinacy of love, every day to discern his voice, through human beings and events, and if we unceasingly follow in his footsteps, how can we fail to enter through the gate?

We will thus verify in our life, and fully realize, the name by which his love has named each one of us. A love proved and sealed by death, so that we might have life and have it abundantly.

# Fifth Sunday of Easter

## John 14:1-12

*When Jesus was about to pass from this world to the Father, he said to his disciples, "Do not let your hearts be troubled. You have faith in God, have faith also in me. In my Father's house, there are many dwelling places. If there were not, would I have told you that I am going to prepare a place for you? And if I go to prepare a place for you, I will come back again and take you to myself, so that where I am, you also may be with me. Where I am going, you know the way." Thomas said to him, "Lord, we do not know where you are going. How can we know the way?" Jesus answered him, "I am the Way, the Truth, and the Life. No one comes to the Father except through me. If you knew me, you would also know my Father. From now on, you do know him and have seen him." Philip said to him, "Lord, show us the Father, and that will be enough for us." Jesus said to him in reply, "Have I been with you for so long a time, Philip, and you still do not know me? Whoever has seen me has seen the Father. How can you say to me, 'Show us the Father'? Do you not then believe that I am in the Father and the Father is in me? The words that I speak to you, I do not speak on my own. The Father who remains in me is doing his works. Believe me that I am in the Father and the Father is in me, or, if you do not believe my words, believe because of the works themselves. Amen, amen, I say to you: whoever believes in me will do the works that I do and will do greater works than these, because I am going to the Father.*

For a long time, the disciples had accompanied Jesus, grown accustomed to the features of his face—but without really knowing it. His face was more than that of a man; it was, in all truth, the face of God. "Philip, whoever has seen me has seen the Father. . . . Do you not believe that I am in the Father, and the Father is in me?" To live on intimate terms with Jesus, to rub shoulders with him day after day, had therefore not been sufficient. And as for us, twenty centuries later, how are we to recognize Jesus and see the Father?

Physical proximity had been of no use to the disciples. Our proximity with Jesus is different; it is given us by the Spirit. Since the moment of our baptism, we bear the features of Jesus' countenance stamped on our hearts. Not the exterior form of his visage, the color of his eyes or of his hair, but his true face, the eternal face of the Risen One from beyond this world.

Day after day, patiently, tenderly, the Spirit marks and embellishes it with these features: an interior, hidden icon of Jesus, bearing an ever greater and more ravishing likeness. Every word of the Gospel that is heard, savored, and assimilated imprints it more faithfully upon our heart. Every word of Jesus is projected onto a picture adorned with colors in the depths of our being, there where his face becomes ever more recognizable to our eyes, but only to the eyes of our heart.

Thanks to this interior icon, we are in a position to recognize Jesus in exterior icons, in the masterpieces of our Christian iconographers. It is the inner icon that makes our heart quiver when it is presented with some portrait of

Jesus. Innumerable are these images, these holy Faces of Jesus, in every epoch, in all styles and cultures, from the majestic Pantocrator of Byzantium to the sorrowful Christ of Rouault. So unalike, in one sense, and yet perfectly recognizable, and even downright similar since, thanks to our inner icon, we identify everywhere, and with equal assurance, the one visage of Jesus of which no icon made by human hands could express all the beauty.

The same holds true of the presence of Jesus in the sacraments. This is because we no longer know Jesus according to the flesh (2 Cor 5:16), but only according to his features that the Spirit has traced in our heart and that we perceive in the liturgical signs as well as in the splendor of creation. Also, in the beauty of the face of a man or of a woman, a masterpiece of iconography, traced in the image and likeness of Jesus.

In the beauty of human beings, yes, but also in their ugliness, their poverty, their distress. In the humble and littlest ones, of whom Jesus said that in them it is he whom people stare at, him whom they welcome (Mark 9:36). He whose face became truly unrecognizable at the hour of his passion, wounded and disfigured by our sins. Since then, there is no human countenance, however ravaged by evil and moral depravity, upon which Jesus' own face has not left some trace. No man or woman in whom, trembling with joy and love, we could not descry the icon of Jesus.

This is so, always thanks to the interior icon of Jesus that the Spirit draws in our heart! It is this icon also that, on the faces of the saints, or on the face of one of our brothers or sisters approaching the moment of death, suddenly manifests itself with a beauty that comes from elsewhere. The same icon that renders so serene and calm certain faces of the deceased who have just fallen asleep in Jesus.

To fall asleep in him and, suddenly, to recognize him for good. For it is at the moment of death that the image of him that we bear in our heart will allow us to recognize Jesus immediately. And we will see him with our own eyes, such as he is: the most beautiful of the children of men, the human face of God. It is indeed he who is our Way, our Truth, and our Life (John 14:6). And it is by way of him that we go to the Father (Matt 11:27).

# Sixth Sunday of Easter

## John 14:15-21

*At the hour when Jesus was to pass from this world to the Father, he said to his disciples, "If you love me, you will keep my commandments. And I will ask the Father, and he will give you another Advocate to be with you always, the Spirit of truth that the world cannot receive because it neither sees nor knows it. But you know it because it remains with you and will be in you. I will not leave you orphans; I will come to you. In a little while, the world will no longer see me, but you will see me, because I live and you too will live. On that day, you will know that I am in my Father, and you are in me, and I in you. Whoever has received my commandments and keeps them is the one who loves me. And whoever loves me will be loved by my Father, and I will love him and will reveal myself to him."*

"If you love me." Jesus does not hesitate to speak with great directness, employing words that we would pronounce only with extreme reserve. "I love you." "Do you love me?" We spontaneously surround this verb, perhaps the most important one in our lexicon, with great modesty. Jesus, by contrast, establishes himself squarely within our most intimate sentiments. He feels at home there and dares to claim these feelings for himself: "If you love me."

How are we to respond to this direct demand on the part of Jesus? Are we sure that we really love him, or even that we want to love him? Jesus offers us a criterion for this love: "Keep my commandments." And a few verses later: "Whoever has accepted my commandments and keeps them is the one who loves me."

My commandments? Which commandments? The word *commandment* lends itself to confusion. In the mouth of Jesus, it surely does not include the thousand and one prescriptions of the old law, against which he unceasingly rose up. The Torah has become in Jesus a new Torah, a new commandment, which definitively fulfills the Law and the prophets. But Jesus often inculcates in us this new commandment: "I give you a new Law: love one another as I have loved you" (John 13:34).

Thus Jesus' injunction becomes very simple and his request of love transparent: "If you love me, love one another as I have loved you." Jesus invites us to enter upon a marvelous adventure in which the verb *to love* is conjugated in all its forms. A veritable circle of love: to love, to be loved, to love one another.

How to enter this circle? Is it arduous, this new commandment? The surprising thing: it is not up to us to enter it. It is Jesus who comes to meet us, who makes himself a beggar of our love. Saint John is explicit on this point: "Love consists in this: not that we have loved God, but that he loved us first" (1 John 4:10). The "if you love me," in the mouth of Jesus, thus signifies, "If you have let yourselves be loved by me, then you have been able to discover my love." This is, in addition, the obvious condition for fulfilling the new commandment, which consists precisely in loving others as Jesus has loved us. How can we do this if we have never experienced to what an extent we are loved by him?

In the face of this experience, Jesus has not left us on our own. He has just promised us an Advocate, the Holy Spirit of truth. He himself is the love and the gentleness of Jesus within us. The world will not recognize or see it because the world has not entered this mysterious circle of love. But, as for us, we recognize it—Jesus affirms this strongly—because it lives in us and remains with us.

There is still more. Since we are thus bathed in love, Jesus will no longer be absent to us. He is absent to "the world" in its incapacity to see him, but not to those who love him, because they have been loved by him: "But you will see me," Jesus affirms, "because I live and you also will live." We will even sense how Jesus is from now on with his Father, in the same way that we are always with him and he with us.

This circle of love will never come to an end. At length, the Father himself will enter it, for "whoever loves me," Jesus declares, "will be loved by my Father, and I will love him and reveal myself to him." This final unveiling of the whole Jesus is the one thing we lack here below. We love Jesus but without yet seeing him. Joy and suffering at the same time. From time to time, a liturgy, or someone's face, or the spiritual splendor of an icon, will lift a corner of the veil to the point of moving us to tears and making us want to see at once the tearing of that veil that still impedes the encounter, that we might at last know all the love with which he loves us.

# Ascension

Matthew 28:16-20

*The Eleven journeyed to Galilee, to the mountain to which Jesus had ordered them. When they saw him, they worshiped him, but some doubted. Jesus approached them and addressed them in these words: "All authority in heaven and on earth has been handed over to me. Go, therefore, and make disciples of all nations, baptizing them in the name of the Father, and of the Son, and of the Holy Spirit, and teaching them to keep all the commandments that I have given you. And behold, I am with you always, until the end of the world."*

When, forty days after his resurrection, Jesus arranges a rendezvous with his disciples on a hill in Galilee, the latter must have understood instinctively that an important event was going to take place, an event about which they had divergent feelings. Some of them, says the Gospel, already believed in Jesus and worshiped him; others entertained doubts about him. Some were even completely mistaken about him, according to Luke's testimony: they had the boldness to ask their Messiah whether the time had finally come for the restorations of sovereignty to Israel.

What is happening is of an entirely different order. After a few words that are understood by all as a farewell address,

Jesus is taken from them, and a cloud removes him from their sight. In the Bible, the cloud always signifies the divine; it is Jesus' humanity that withdraws, provisionally concealing itself in his divinity.

Jesus' human form has, in fact, withdrawn from them. The disciples have no doubt about this, and it has left them all sad and distraught. A final word from Jesus nevertheless fills them with a tenuous hope, a mysterious word that seems to contradict the event that has just transpired: "Behold, I am with you always, until the end of the world." A promise as astonishing as it is insistent: until the end of time, at no moment either of their lives or of the subsequent history of the world, will Jesus ever be lacking to them. He will remain there, not only as a presence in their minds but, it seems, with a most concrete sort of presence: "I will be with you always."

There is yet more, but the disciples cannot understand it for the moment. They will understand in a few days when another promise is realized. Jesus' presence and proximity in their midst will be such that they will be able to bear witness to it, to carry his message, to announce the good news in his name, and to transmit to the entire world that baptism in the Spirit that they are on the point of receiving.

It is in this power from on high, in the Holy Spirit, that Jesus will henceforth be present to them, more evident and more efficacious than ever. Jesus will remind them that it is precisely this that he had promised them even if, at the time, they hardly understood what he was trying to tell them. The Gospel of John, the beloved disciple, who divined more than the others, will magnificently disclose Jesus' promise: the Spirit will complete Jesus' work (John 16:13-15); what he does or says will be taken from Jesus; he will remind the disciples of, and clarify for them, whatever Jesus had told them during his life and had remained opaque until then, precisely because the Spirit had not yet been given to them (John 7:39).

There is something still more marvelous and comforting. While they are absorbed in watching the traces of Jesus disappear in the sky, two angels appear to them, again bearing better tidings. Jesus has left them, of course, but not forever. One day, he will come back in just the same way that they have seen him depart, that is, in the glory of his transfigured humanity. They have lost nothing definitively. The same beloved face, the same hands—pierced through yet saving and healing—the same gentle but irresistible gaze, will be restored to them finally and forever.

The time that now opens before them, and before us as well, is the time of the church that continues to this day. Jesus was here once, and we live from his memory transmitted by the eyewitnesses. But he is always and at every hour with us still, causing us to relive—through his Spirit and in his Word—all the events of his earthly life, including his Easter. Then he will one day return in glory and, on the strength of his having ceaselessly accompanied all the days of our life, we will recognize him at once. For as of now, we already know him by faith more than we dare to suppose.

# Seventh Sunday of Easter

## John 17:1-11

*At the hour when Jesus was to pass from this world to the Father, he raised his eyes to heaven and prayed in these words: "Father, the hour has come. Glorify your son, that your son may glorify you. Thus, as you have given him authority over all flesh, he may give eternal life to those you have given him. And this is eternal life: to know you, the only true God, and the one whom you sent, Jesus Christ.*

*"I have glorified you on earth by accomplishing the work that you gave me to do. Now do you, Father, glorify me with you with the glory that I had with you before the world began. I made known your name to those you have taken out of the world and given to me. They belonged to you, and you gave them to me, and they have kept your word. And they have understood that everything you gave me comes from you; for I gave them the words that you gave me, and they accepted them and truly understood that I came from you, and they have believed that you sent me.*

*"I pray for them. I do not pray for the world but for those you have given me. They are yours, and everything that is mine is yours, and everything that is yours is mine, and I have been glorified in them. Now I am no longer in the world, but they are in the world, and I am coming to you."*

"They belong to you." When Jesus speaks of us to his Father, this is how he designates us: the ones who belong to him. Only Jesus fully experiences what that means in the concrete. In the strictest possible sense, Jesus belongs to the Father. He is born of him, has come from him (John 16:28), was sent by him (John 3:17); he speaks the words he has received from him (John 3:24); he accomplishes his works (John 5:19). The Father and he are one (John 10:30) to such an extent that whoever sees Jesus has seen the Father (John 14:9).

When Jesus says that we belong to his Father, he says at the same time that we belong to him, Jesus, as well. At the moment when Jesus became man, he received as it were the whole human race as a gift from the Father. In fact, when he addresses his Father he calls us "those you have taken out of the world and given to me." If we are still "in the world," as Jesus also says to him, we are nonetheless already "taken out of the world" so that we might truly belong to Jesus.

For what reason has the Father taken us out of the world? By a completely gratuitous choice, a choice of love, for a reason that reason cannot comprehend, except that it is the Father's desire to be loved in turn, since no one, not even God, wants to be alone in loving. But this desire of the Father could not be realized except in Jesus and in the love with which Jesus came to envelop us.

In his prayer, Jesus reminds his Father, "I made known your name to those you have given to me." This revelation was not simple. It was necessary for the apostles to rub shoulders with Jesus for a long time, to be initially mistaken about his identity, to become distressed witnesses of his death, to doubt again before the growing evidence of his resurrection, until finally divining, behind Jesus, him whom he presented to them as being "my Father and your Father" (John 20:17). At the hour when Jesus is at the point of leaving them, it is a done deal: "They have understood that all that you gave me comes from you, and they have truly understood that I came from you."

Jesus is our way to the Father, because there is no other way. "No one comes to the Father except through me," Jesus affirms (John 14:6). In addition, no one can come to Jesus "unless the Father who sent me draw him" (John 6:44). It is the Father in person who sets us on the way of Jesus, a way on which it is impossible not to meet him. For in belonging to Jesus, we belong also to his Father. "They belong to you," Jesus prays, "and everything that is mine is yours, as everything that is yours is mine." Jesus' disciples are like the mutual love of the Father and the Son, the bond of their love. For all that is exterior to the trinitarian communion, it is in us that the Father and the Son encounter and love each other, and without us they could not love each other. To so great a degree do we belong to the one and to the other!

That is why Jesus asks his Father to give him the glory that he had with him before the foundation of the world, that he might share it with his own, that is, with those who belong to the Father, since they already belong to him as well.

That is also why Jesus asks eternal life for them. This is the life that he himself is—"I am the life" (John 11:25)—and that he came into the world to offer: "I came so that they might have life and have it abundantly" (John 10:10). Well, this eternal life is precisely "to know you, the only true God, and the one whom you sent, Jesus Christ," and to belong thereby to the Father and to the Son, as the fruit of their love, the bond between them, and their glory always and forever.

# Pentecost

John 20:19-23

*On the first day of the week, when the disciples were gathered together behind locked doors for fear of the Jews, Jesus came and stood in their midst and said, "Peace be with you." When he had said this, he showed them his hands and his side. The disciples rejoiced when they saw the Lord.*

*Jesus said to them again, "Peace be with you. As the Father has sent me, so I send you." Then he breathed on them and said, "Receive the Holy Spirit. Whose sins you forgive are forgiven them, whose sins you retain are retained."*

"A great noise, like that of a strong, driving wind": it is in these terms that Luke describes the descent of the Spirit upon the apostles. That happened once, long ago. And today, where is the Spirit in our church? Where does it still act in this explosive fashion, thundering, dividing in tongues of fire, recreating the hearts of disciples, stirring up unheard of fervor and audacity in the church?

Where are the miracles that once took place? Has the Spirit hidden himself from that time on? And if so, why? Or have we perhaps become so accustomed to the Spirit's presence that he now passes us by unnoticed? Has the Spirit of Jesus become discreet, effaced, practically voiceless? The same Spirit as ever, to be sure, but unbeknownst to us?

Brothers and sisters, there can be no doubt about it: the Holy Spirit is still at work among us. Pentecost is not merely yesterday's event, a memory that we commemorate but whose echo fades with the passing of the years. On the contrary, it is always present, renewed at every instant, and the Spirit's action, far from growing lukewarm, becomes more and more insistent, increasingly marvelous and unpredictable.

If, *per impossibile*, the Spirit had abandoned the church, we would not be here right now, for nothing would have drawn us to this place. "No one comes to me, unless the Father who sent me draw him" (John 6:44), said Jesus. And our faith in Jesus would no longer be faith, but only some sort of sincere pagan wisdom, a body of probabilities or likelihoods, more or less intellectually convincing but in no way contagious or desirable. And our beloved Jesus, our brother and our God, would no longer be anything but one celebrity among so many others; a great man, certainly, perhaps a superman, impressive but not at all attractive or lovable. Saint Paul already reminded us: "Brothers and sisters, apart from the Holy Spirit, no one can say: Jesus is Lord" (1 Cor 12:3).

But above all, if the Holy Spirit were not continually with us, and even in us, if he did not—according to Jesus' promise—inhabit us, our weaknesses would be immediately fatal, our interior wounds without hope of healing, and the weight of our sins would become more unbearable day by day. "Receive the Holy Spirit," Jesus said to his apostles. "Whose sins you forgive are forgiven them" (John 20:22). The nascent confidence that rises up in our hearts sometimes in the midst of temptations and adversity, that is the Spirit at work; the humble source of surrender and of peace that wells up within us at the heart of the trial is, again, the Spirit; but above all, the sweet joy of the sinner who knows and feels himself forgiven and loved more than ever after his fault, and even because of his fault, that too is the work of the Spirit.

For it is chiefly joy, nothing more and nothing less, the joy of our origins and our depths, the very joy of God himself, that is hidden behind all the superficial delights that assail us from all sides and easily distract us from God. And because it is God's joy, the Spirit does not frighten, but attracts us. It never threatens, but it reassures us. It does not accuse, but it pardons us. It constrains no one, but rather it seduces us. It does not coerce, but it tames us and takes us by the hand with infinite tact and gentleness. For it is the kindness and tenderness of God spread abroad unceasingly throughout the world and into our hearts.

Finally, the Spirit is desire and prayer, the most audacious desire that can inhabit a human being, the most irresistible prayer that is hidden in the heart. We know it by experience, and Saint Paul recalls it to us: "We do not know how to pray as we ought. But the Spirit comes to the aid of our weakness with ineffable groanings, crying ceaselessly in our heart: Abba, Father" (Rom 8:26). And there, in our heart, he intercedes for the whole universe. Brothers and sisters, it suffices that a believer open the interior ear, capture this prayer of the Spirit within, and make it one's own, for the whole world to be touched by it as by a new Pentecost.

# Trinity Sunday

## John 16:12-15

*At the hour when he was to pass from this world to the Father, Jesus said to his disciples, "I have much more to tell you, but you cannot bear it now. But when he comes, the Spirit of truth, he will lead you into all truth. He will not speak on his own, but he will speak what he hears and make known to you the things that are to come. He will glorify me, for he will take from what is mine and declare it to you. All that the Father has is mine; for this reason I have said to you that he will take from what is mine and declare it to you."*

The mystery of the Trinity is at once near and distant. First, it is near, since as of our baptism we have been plunged with eyes closed, so to speak, into the love of the Father, the Son, and the Holy Spirit, but without understanding much of it—and with good reason. To the extent that the years have passed and we have been exposed to catechesis upon catechesis, explanation upon explanation, the mystery has hardly been clarified before the eyes of our heart so slow to believe, that is, a heart that needs a lot of time—perhaps even a whole lifetime—to savor and deepen its faith a little.

This is not a reproach. Jesus himself explicitly told his apostles that he had many things to tell them that they were not yet capable of understanding (John 16:12). Among these things that we are for the moment or, in some cases, for a long time incapable of understanding, there is surely the mystery of the Trinity. We don't understand it, yet we believe in the Father, the Son, and the Holy Spirit, one only God in three Persons. But we feel at the same time that this perfectly correct formulation of the catechism will never suffice to embrace the mystery that it attempts to convey. Such formulas are at once indispensable and insufficient, merely rough sketches of the mystery, corresponding to the measure of our limited conceptions.

In fact, it is not in the domain of concepts that the density of the mystery will be little by little revealed to us. It is in the measure that we ourselves penetrate therein that the life of the Trinity will affect us, draw us into the interior of its mystery, ravished as we may one day be by God in person, if only we truly desire it.

The paths of approach to this mystery are diverse because our personal vocations differ likewise. Each one of us, however, has a unique way to enter into relationship with one of the three Persons, and by the mediation of that Person with the other two as well.

Maybe it is first of all the face of the Father of all kindness that has one day stood out from behind that impersonal and distant God of whom everyone speaks only to affirm or to deny him. An incomparable Father whose love never takes offense, who abides in patience, who awaits his hour, who forgives incessantly. No longer an abstract God, or even an absent God, but a Father who takes me into his care and with whom, in moments of peace and surrender as well as in moments of great distress, I can converse intimately like a child with his father.

A Father who loved us so much that he sent us his only Son, as the Gospel has just reminded us, so that not one of us may be lost. For where the Father is recognized, the Son is not far away. Their mutual likeness is so much the greater than it would be according to that perfectly absurd hypothesis according to which the Father would have become incarnate at the same time as his Son, and the two would be in every respect identical, distinguishable only by the gaze that each would bear towards the other. On the one side, the Father's gaze full of loving pride; on the other, the affectionate and trusting look of the Son. But such a hypothesis is totally absurd precisely because the Father did not want any human face but that of the Son: "The Father and I are one. . . . Whoever has seen me has seen the Father" (John 10:30; 14:9).

However, Jesus was not ready to provide us with the last word on this mystery. He left that to the Holy Spirit: "When the Spirit of truth comes, he will lead you to all truth" (John 16:13). The Spirit does not instruct us with a catechetical supplement. He teaches us completely otherwise, by an interior unction, as Saint John says (1 John 2:20-27), by a sweetness at the boundaries of the perceptible, a secret delight that he pours into our hearts to enable us to taste the things of God. Here below, his ministry is only beginning, and until the end of our earthly life we will not have advanced beyond stammering about the things of God. Eternity itself will not suffice us . . . or rather, it will draw us ever more deeply into the ineffable mystery of the one love in three Persons. We will then advance from discovery to discovery, to comprehend ever more clearly the mystery of the Trinity, "that which eye has not seen, ear has not heard, what has never entered the human heart, what God has prepared for those who love him" (1 Cor 2:9).

## Second Sunday of Ordinary Time

### John 1:29-34

*When John the Baptist saw Jesus coming towards him, he said, "Behold the Lamb of God, who takes away the sin of the world: he it was of whom I said that a man is coming after me who ranks ahead of me, because he existed before me. I did not know him, but the reason I came baptizing with water was so that he might be made known to Israel." John also testified and said, "I saw the Spirit come down from heaven like a dove and remain upon him. I did not know him, but the one who sent me to baptize with water said to me, 'On whomever you see the Spirit come down and remain, he it is who will baptize with the Holy Spirit.' Now I have seen and testified that he is the Son of God."*

John the Baptist attests that he recognized Jesus. Until now, he had not known him; from now on, he does. The one who had sent him revealed to him by what sign Jesus would be recognizable: "On whomever you see the Spirit come down and remain." And in fact, John testifies to this: "I have seen the Spirit come down from heaven like a dove and remain upon him." Jesus himself, when he speaks in a synagogue for the first time, will invoke the Spirit: "The Spirit of the Lord is upon me. He has sent me to proclaim Good News to the poor" (Luke 4:18).

This companionship, this intimacy between Jesus and the Spirit, does not go back only to some point in Jesus' earthly life. It always pre-existed in eternity at the heart of the Trinity, in the bosom of the Father. The Spirit being the love, the indissoluble bond between the Father and the Son, he could not fail to be manifested in this world at the same time as the Son. When the Son takes up the word, the Spirit appears as well, inseparable from the Son who is manifested, glorified, and transfigured.

The Holy Spirit does not keep company with Jesus merely to reveal him to us. He appears with him also on our behalf. As he belongs to Jesus, he belongs to us also, for he is the unheard-of gift that Jesus has come to bring us—"Receive the Holy Spirit" (John 20:23)—the gift thanks to which our sins are forgiven and we have become, in our turn, sons and daughters of the same Father. "The proof that you are sons," says Saint Paul, "is that we have received of his Spirit, no longer a Spirit of slavery, but a Spirit of freedom, the Spirit of the Son who cries out in our hearts: Abba, Father!" (Rom 8:15). Upon us also the Spirit has descended and remains.

This took place effectively for us, just as for Jesus, at the time of our baptism, invisibly, but very truly, although only in the form of a seed called to develop. That is why the Spirit does not cease to come to us, every day. He sticks to our heart, literally, even if we remain unaware of him. He moves within us, vivifies us. He is our assiduous and faithful companion at every moment. Without him, we would know nothing of Jesus except what the books say of him, nor would we know him in our brothers and sisters. According to Saint Paul, we could not even say "Jesus is Lord" unless he so inspired us (1 Cor 12:3).

His presence in us is nevertheless fragile, vulnerable. We could turn a deaf ear to him, sadden him, even—as Saint Paul also says—extinguish him (1 Thess 5:19), for he will not force us. Jesus even mentions a sin against the Holy

Spirit that would be the worst sin of all and never be forgiven (Matt 12:31); on all evidence, that is probably because it is he himself, the Holy Spirit, who is our forgiveness. Whoever would set themselves against him have already departed from the ambit of God's love and mercy. To feel the Spirit within us, nothing is more helpful than becoming aware of our own needs. He dwells within our poverty. It is he alone who heals our wounds in depth. Was he not given us to compensate for Jesus' absence? "If I do not go away," said Jesus, "the Spirit will not come to you" (John 16:7). He does not replace Jesus, but he consoles us in his absence. He recalls him to us and enables us to know him profoundly (John 16:13). Above all, he confirms us in our afflictions. It is thanks to him that we are at our strongest precisely when we are most beset by weakness. For it is indeed the Holy Spirit who comes to the aid of our weakness, even in our incapacity to pray. "For we do not know how to pray as we ought," again says Saint Paul, "but the Spirit intercedes for us" (Rom 8:26).

And as it was the Spirit who once enabled John the Baptist to recognize Jesus, it is likewise he who enables us today to recognize each other as brothers and sisters, children of the same Father: the Spirit who is himself the love with which we love one another, as Jesus has loved us.

# Third Sunday of Ordinary Time

## Matthew 4:17-23

*From that time one, Jesus began to proclaim, "Repent, for the kingdom of heaven is at hand!"*

*As he was walking along the Sea of Galilee, he saw two brothers, Simon, who is called Peter, and his brother Andrew, casting their nets into the sea: they were fishermen. Jesus said to them, "Come after me, and I will make you fishers of people." So they at once left their nets and followed him. A little farther on, he saw two other brothers, James the son of Zebedee, and his brother John, who were in a boat with their father, mending their nets. He called them, and immediately they left the boat and their father and followed him.*

*Jesus went throughout all of Galilee, teaching in their synagogues, proclaiming the Gospel of the kingdom, and healing every disease and illness among the people.*

The four future apostles are engaged in their work. Jesus passes their way: a gaze, a word, and behold, the four commit themselves to his following. Their profession, the instruments of their labor, even their father—these no longer carry any weight, it seems. Suddenly, they are as it were sucked in, snatched up by this unexpected and still unknown passerby. To two of them, indeed, Jesus has let a vague promise shine forth: "I will make you fishers of people." For the moment, they have surely not understood. And there is nothing else: no contract, no promised salary, no vision of a future, nothing.

The suddenness of such vocations never ceases to astonish us, and it even raises some questions. Few actions are as spontaneous as the response to Jesus' call in the gospels. No one reasons it out, no one weighs the pros and the cons, no one counts the cost. They simply leave everything and follow Jesus.

To what end? In the pursuit of what goal? Jesus has said nothing, and it does not seem even to have occurred to them to ask Jesus for an explanation. Besides, it is not any goal or plan that has thus shaken them out of their routine, but only Jesus himself: his person and his imperious desire for them to follow him, to stay where he stays, sufficed for them.

On the apostles' side, it surely requires a bit of ingenuousness and innocence, a heart and mind still virginal and available, for them so to hasten toward the offer set before them almost like a subtly arranged trap. But that too suffices. In fact, it is not they themselves who are operative here, extracting from themselves some sorrowful and generous consent. Jesus is at work, alone and sovereign. The disciples succumb to his influence, but with complete freedom, in the sense that they acquiesce to the call received and embrace it.

Such a sudden fervor for Jesus, as instantaneous as it is inexplicable, has a name: thunderclap. An amazing charm must have been at work in Jesus, not to hold the disciples in his power or to subject them to his orders, but to engender in their hearts equally marvelous desire. They hadn't known for what they were truly hungry and thirsty, something infinitely more satisfying than their boat and their nets. They had not known the extent to which they were wounded, nor what sort of love would one day be needed to heal such a wound. A mere look, a mere word from Jesus touched the wound, and it started to hurt again. But at the same moment, in this look, beyond these words, they glimpsed the only one who could heal them definitively. Then, as if by instinct and unreflectively, they accepted the cost, they abandoned everything to follow him, sold everything to gain him alone.

The thunderclap is but the first step in a long adventure. It must fizzle out, for it isn't meant to endure. It will inexorably fade and even die, so that the flowers and fruits of which it is merely the herald may bloom and ripen. Even the apostles will have to learn this firsthand. They will grow discouraged in Jesus' company, will misunderstand him, will protest. One sad spring evening, they will run off while their beloved is led away, taken prisoner by the soldiers. Three years of public ministry with Jesus will not have been enough to strengthen their love permanently. On Easter night, they will still doubt, refusing to lend credence to the tales of women (Luke 24:22).

Left to itself, their initial thunderclap would have remained sterile. That it might become an everlasting love, it needed also the morning of Pentecost and its power from on high: the Holy Spirit, sent by Jesus, the very love of God henceforth poured out into their hearts. The fire of their first love might have cooled or even been extinguished. What does it matter? A new fire would come to embrace their hearts, one that would never be put out, a fire by which all their brothers and sisters might in turn be warmed and embraced.

## Fourth Sunday of Ordinary Time

Matthew 5:1-12a

*When Jesus saw the crowd that had followed him, he went up the mountain. He sat down, and his disciples approached him. Then he opened his mouth and began to teach them, saying,*

*Blessed the poor in spirit: the kingdom of heaven is theirs.*

*Blessed are the meek, for they will inherit the earth.*

*Blessed are they who mourn, for they will be comforted.*

*Blessed are they who hunger and thirst for righteousness, for they will be satisfied.*

*Blessed are the pure of heart, for they shall see God.*

*Blessed are the peacemakers, for they shall be called children of God.*

*Blessed are they who are persecuted for the sake of righteousness, for the kingdom of heaven is theirs.*

*Blessed are you when they insult you, and persecute you, and utter every kind of evil against you falsely because of me. Rejoice and be glad, for your reward will be great in heaven.*

"The kingdom of heaven is at hand" is the message that Jesus preaches everywhere. But for whom is this kingdom intended? Where and how can it be discovered? And each of us is tempted to add, "And will I too be its happy beneficiary?" It is to all these questions that Jesus wants to offer a response, at the debut of his ministry, by means of what have conventionally been called the Beatitudes.

Some have understood them to be commandments: the Beatitudes would then be the Decalogue of the New Covenant, and the keeping of them the requirement for entry into the kingdom. Others regard them as a synthesis of the more perfect morality that Jesus came to supply. It is possible to read them in this fashion. Probably, however, they are quite simply an ensemble of signs, indications, one could even say symptoms, that Jesus puts at the service of his disciples: symptoms thanks to which each of us can recognize whether the good news of the kingdom has really made its home in us.

In fact, it pertains indubitably to the good news. Jesus proclaims blessedness: "Blessed the poor, blessed the meek," and this good news does not chiefly have in view the elaboration of a body of doctrine, nor the reform of an ethical code, but is addressed to each of us personally: "You, how blessed you are, if such a sign of the kingdom makes itself felt in your heart!"

Yet, to our surprise, this blessedness of the kingdom is always linked, through its symptoms, either to some kind of misfortune here below, such as poverty, tears, hunger and thirst, persecutions, or to attitudes that don't pay in this world, such as meekness, mercy, the ministry of reconciliation—attitudes that often even turn against those who think they must adopt them.

It is as if the kingdom of Jesus cannot be glimpsed except through a certain hollow of human existence, through a void that is waiting to be filled, as if it were kept hidden behind a feeling of destitution, of need, that we fail to identify on the first attempt. As Jesus said: through a hunger and thirst for righteousness—that is, in biblical language, a still vague hunger and thirst for holiness.

O blessed poverty! blessed hunger and blessed thirst, for which moreover Jesus offers us his felicitations, since in them there appear to us even now, in the form of a void, the future delights and refreshments of the kingdom. These mysterious voids in our life, sometimes experienced as acutely painful, yet accepted and offered up to God, become for each one of us the sure sign that the kingdom of Jesus is knocking at the door of our heart, and that we are among those made blessed by his call.

But that holds true only on the condition that we are able to identify these voids, that we allow ourselves to feel them and even to suffer through and weep over them: "Blessed are they who mourn, for they will be comforted." Alas, we sometimes shrink back in fear from these lacunae, to such a degree that we end by covering them up more or less convincingly. So much conversation (even edifying), so many impressive gesticulations, so many well-meaning commitments are there principally to make us forget the emptiness that so terribly pains us and that in addition discredits us in the eyes of a world that we were claiming to win for Christ. How irritating it is to accept the signs of the kingdom that Paul enumerates in the second reading: "God has chosen what the world considers foolish, what it considers weak, what is despised, what counts for nothing."

To perceive these signs in the depths of the heart, to feel the extent to which we are poor and weak, and that without Jesus we can do nothing—that is the grace of all graces. This is the true poverty, our only wealth, upon which the future kingdom depends: "Blessed the poor in spirit, for the kingdom of heaven is theirs."

# Fifth Sunday of Ordinary Time

Matthew 5:13-16

*When the disciples had gathered around Jesus on the mountain, he said to them,*

*"You are the salt of the earth. But if salt becomes insipid, with what can it be made salty again? It is no good for anything except to be thrown out and trampled underfoot.*

*"You are the light of the world. A city set upon a hill cannot be hidden. Nor does one light a lamp and put it under a basket; it is put on a lampstand, so that it may give light to all in the house. In the same way, your light must shine before others, so that they may see your good deeds and glorify your heavenly Father."*

To explain to his disciples what they are at the heart of the world, Jesus employs two simple but suggestive images: they are salt and light, the salt of the earth, the light of the world.

These two images share a common element: they express the absolute necessity for the presence of Christians in the midst of the world: without salt, the world would lose its savor; without light, it would be plunged in darkness. These two images are at the same time complementary; one could even, if necessary, set them in mutual opposition. For salt to spread its flavor, it must be hidden and dissolved in the foods it flavors. Light, by contrast, must be placed on a lampstand to shine before all those who are in the house. Salt is discreet, almost invisible; light shines and demands to be seen, says Jesus, so that people "may see your good deeds and glorify your heavenly Father."

The two images also clarify, in their fashion, the "more" that the faith of Christians brings to the world. As salt of the earth, first, it is the divine condiment that gives to the world its true flavor, that exquisite taste that can only come to it from elsewhere. The Christian is in the position to give it this flavor through his faith, but only because Jesus has first imparted to the world and to all creation his own true taste. It is through him, and for him, that all things have been created, it is in him that all is held in being, it is toward him that all things grow and develop, and it is in him that the whole universe will one day come to fulfillment. The incarnation of the Son of God was the crowning of creation, revealing for us this taste of the world, so refined that it is the very taste of God and that it tells us how greatly God takes pleasure in savoring his creation.

Likewise for the image of light. The faith of Christians is called to bring to light certain aspects of the world that without them would remain forever concealed. Not, of course, on the level of scientific discoveries, the progress of which has become so accelerated in our own day. The light of faith is different. It enables the discovery of another splendor of the world, in its relationship with God and with human beings. It reveals the extent to which it is indwelt, even today, by the Word incarnate, who shines through all the beauty of the world and transfigures it little by little. It manifests itself above all on human faces, all faces, the most attractive as well as the most unsightly, and it teaches how we can there descry what the jaded eye, the carnal eye (as the Bible would say), could never admire. For what the light of faith illuminates it thereby makes lovable, and it enables us to love as God loves.

As with the salt, the Christian is not himself the source of this light. He has it from another, whose illumination he received at the moment of his baptism, from Jesus, who said, "I am the light of the world" (John 8:12), and without which the whole world would lie in darkness.

Salt and light, God's flavor and his brightness—that is what we are, brothers and sisters, without knowing it, and most of the time without having sought for it. How can we be sure of possessing God's flavor within ourselves? For it is possible to taste nothing of it in oneself yet to distill it among others, unbeknownst to us. God works that way, it's his own *savoir faire*. For us, it is enough to remain solidly rooted in Jesus, attached to him, the world's savor and its light. "The one who remains in me will bear much fruit" (John 15:5).

# Sixth Sunday of Ordinary Time

## Matthew 5:17-37

*When the disciples had gathered around Jesus on the mountain, he said to them, "Do not think that I have come to abolish the law or the prophets. I have not come to abolish, but to fulfill them. Amen, I say to you, not one jot or stroke of the law will disappear until all things have been accomplished. Therefore, whoever breaks one of the least of these commandments and teaches others to do the same will be called least in the kingdom of heaven. But whoever observes them and teaches others to do so will be called great in the kingdom of heaven. I tell you, unless your righteousness surpasses that of the scribes and Pharisees, you will not enter the kingdom of heaven.*

*"You have heard that it was said to your ancestors, 'You shall not murder, and whoever murders will be liable to judgment.' But I say to you, whoever is angry with his brother will be liable to judgment. And whoever insults his brother will be liable to the Sanhedrin. And whoever says, 'You fool,' will be liable to the Gehenna of fire. Therefore, if you present your gift at the altar and remember that your brother has something against you, leave your gift there at the altar. Go first and be reconciled with your brother, then come and offer your gift. Come to an agreement with your opponent while on the way to court with him. Otherwise, your opponent will hand you over to the judge, and the*

*judge will hand you over to the guard, and the guard will throw you into prison. Amen, I say to you, you will not be released until you have paid the last penny.*

*"You have heard that it was said, 'You shall not commit adultery.' But I say to you, whoever looks at a woman to lust after her has already committed adultery with her in his heart. If your right eye causes you to sin, pluck it out and throw it away: better for you to lose one of your members than for your whole body to be cast into Gehenna. And if your right hand causes you to sin, cut it off and throw it away: better for you to lose one of your members than for your whole body to go into Gehenna.*

*"Again, it was said: 'if someone separates from his wife, he must give her a bill of divorce.' But I say to you, whoever divorces his wife—except in the case of illegitimate union—causes her to commit adultery. And whoever marries a divorced woman commits adultery.*

*"Again, you have heard that it was said to your ancestors, 'You shall not swear a false oath, but you shall pay your vows to the Lord.' But I say to you, do not swear at all, neither by heaven, which is the throne of God, nor by the earth, which is his footstool, nor by Jerusalem, which is the city of the great king. Do not swear by your head, for you cannot make even one of its hairs white or black. Rather, let your* yes *mean* yes *and your* no *mean* no. *Anything else is from the evil one."*

There is a kind of perfection that stops halfway, without reaching the end: "If your righteousness does not surpass that of the scribes and Pharisees, you will not enter the kingdom of heaven," Jesus has just warned us.

Not that their righteousness was lacking in sincerity or generosity. On the contrary, it was abounding in them and, with that, would gladly have imposed itself on others. It preaches a rigorous observance, nitpicking. It multiplies precepts and usages—an intolerable burden, Jesus will say—so as to complicate considerably the life of the pious Jew, investing his universe with a fear of doing evil. Jesus will often meet the adepts of this sort of righteousness, and the encounters will usually be disagreeable. For the Pharisees are quick to establish themselves as judges of others, especially of Jesus and of his disciples. They monitor his behavior. They cover him with reproaches: not fasting according to the prescribed conditions, letting himself be touched by a prostitute, healing someone on the Sabbath. In the end, they will accuse him of blasphemy—he calls himself the Son of God—they will cry out for his death.

Here are two ways of perfection so radically opposed to each other that the one who settles for the first one cannot enter the kingdom of Jesus. But how can we determine where these two ways, so apparently similar at the outset, split off from each other in the concrete conditions of life?

In reality, before diverging, they work together toward common objects. To refrain from killing a brother, to avoid committing adultery—these pertain to the one path as well as to the other. Neither the Pharisee nor the disciple of Jesus is ever dispensed from them. And yet that is not enough for Jesus. Morally upright conduct can pull the wool over one's eyes. It remains on the exterior of the disciple who applies himself to its observance, but, left to itself, it is incapable of healing the heart. But it is precisely the heart that is sick, for it is from the heart—says Jesus—that the sins committed exteriorly derive (Matt 15:18). Even if the façade is more or less happily maintained, the hidden source may remain sullied. It's no use cleansing the outside of the cup, Jesus reminds us, if its contents are an abomination. One day, he will even raise his voice, denouncing the "morally correct" who do not find favor in his eyes: "Whitewashed tombs!" he will hurl at the Pharisees, whose walls alone are shining, but who are filled with corruption within (Matt 23:27).

What matters to Jesus is the heart's healing. Yet to want to be healed, it is first necessary to know, and to accept, that we are sick, whereas the moral astuteness of the Pharisee, and his illusion, is precisely to content himself with an external conformity with the law, and thus to conceal, chiefly from his own eyes, the sickness that gnaws at his heart. What good is it to be outwardly irreproachable if covetousness and hatred find a comfortable abode within? "This people honors me with their lips, but their hearts are far from me," Jesus will reproach the Pharisees (Matt 15:8).

Can we know whether our heart is sick or in good health? Jesus has just given us an infallible criterion: the quality of our relations with others. These relations really demand more than the simple requirement of respecting others' lives or not getting angry with them. They demand that we become capable of feeling whether a brother or sister has something against us even when we are not conscious of any fault on our part. And this exigency is so absolute that it orders even our relations with God: "If you remember that your brother has something against you, leave your gift and go first and be reconciled with him."

An absolute requirement, but so often difficult to put into practice. For the fulfillment thereof, our heart itself will never suffice. What we need is God's heart, his Holy Spirit, he who is the only law of the kingdom. All other sins against the commandments, without exception, will be forgiven, Jesus assures us, but not the sin against the Spirit—that is, against love, the love of God poured into our hearts by the Spirit who has been given us (Rom 5:5).

## Seventh Sunday of Ordinary Time

### Matthew 5:38-48

*When the disciples had gathered around Jesus on the mountain, he said to them, "You have heard that it was said: an eye for an eye, and a tooth for a tooth. But I say to you, offer no resistance to the one who is evil. Rather, if someone strikes you on your right cheek, turn to him the other cheek as well. And if someone goes to law with you over your tunic, give him your cloak as well. And if someone presses you into service for one mile, go with him for two miles. Give to the one who asks of you, and do not turn your back on the one who wants to borrow.*

*"You have heard that it was said: you shall love your neighbor and hate your enemy. But I say to you, love your enemies and pray for those who persecute you. Then you will be children of your Father in heaven, who makes his sun to rise on the bad and the good, and his rain to fall on the just and the unjust. For if you love those who love you, what recompense will you have? Do not the tax collectors do the same? And if you greet your brothers only, what is extraordinary about that? Do not the pagans do the same? So be perfect, just as your heavenly Father is perfect."*

"The pagans and the tax collectors do the same." In Jesus' eyes, this charity does not go far enough. It is not even charity, as he understands it. And yet the pagans do good in their fashion. They are correct, extend friendship to their friends, greet their brothers. They do more than that, especially today, as recent statistics reveal the notable progress of "humanitarian" concerns. From all sides, campaigns of solidarity follow one upon another in soliciting generosity, with proven results. So many miseries are thus effectively relieved. Thanks be to God! Who would dare complain about such a thing?

Jesus too would congratulate our contemporaries, but he would surely add that even this is still not enough, that this level of solidarity is obligatory, the minimum decency required for a beginning of true fraternity among humans, that all human beings without exception are able so to collaborate, and that the least Christians could do would be to devote themselves in the front lines of these endeavors. But finally, that this solidarity is not yet the charity with which he came to set the world aflame and of which a little spark is deposited in the heart of every baptized person. That this charity is an incomparably different thing.

Does this mean that our efforts are not profitable enough, that we must redouble our generosity, that Christians should empty their wallets more than other citizens? Not necessarily. "If I distribute all my goods to the poor," says Saint Paul, "but do not have love—I gain nothing" (1 Cor 13:3). Indeed, we could sincerely distribute all our goods, without truly loving. For love can never be measured in terms of quantities, especially not in quantities of money. Love can only be evaluated by its quality, which cannot be compared to anything and which derives from an order that transcends our simple impulses to generosity. Love is of a quality for which the human heart is always insufficient.

This incomparable character of true charity is expressed by Jesus in the brief sentence that we have just heard, concluding his discourse on love: "So be perfect, just as your heavenly Father is perfect." There is only one who gives us the example of being perfect in love: our Father in heaven. And he does so in multiple ways.

Jesus cites an example from ordinary, common sense. When we speak of charity, we think in terms of equality, of equity. But God is not equitable in love. "He makes his sun to rise on the bad and the good, and his rain to fall on the just and the unjust." His love does not avenge itself on our injustices. It forgives, effaces, and forgets, as if nothing had happened.

There is another example, still more convincing: it is Jesus himself, sent by the Father to reveal to us the only true love. "The proof that God loves us," Saint Paul says, "is that Christ died for us while we were still sinners" (Rom 5:8). His love does not handpick his friends, he does not merely return love for love, he does not select the most meritorious. He includes them all, and he maintains a preferential option for the undeserving, for enemies, for sinners. His love is not reasonable like our generosity, of us who moderate our largesse and give only from our surplus. It is a mad love, so mad that Jesus will one day die of it, die as one counted—in his turn—among sinners (Mark 15:28).

In the life and death of Jesus alone, we can contemplate the face of true love and imitate it from afar, humbly, without ever being discharged of the debt that we owe until death: that of loving our brothers and sisters. What does it matter if we remain forever insolvent in love? Jesus has already paid the debt in our place. He loved us to the end, to the point of handing himself over for us. In his love, we can love in turn: "If he laid down his life for us," says Saint John, "we too ought to lay down our lives for our brothers and sisters" (1 John 3:16).

# Eighth Sunday of Ordinary Time

## Matthew 6:24-34

*When the disciples had gathered around Jesus on the mountain, he said to them, "No one can serve two masters: he will either hate one and love the other, or he will be devoted to one and despise the other. You cannot serve God and mammon. Therefore I say to you, do not worry about your life, what you are to eat, or about your body, what you are to wear. Is not life more than food and the body more than clothing? Look at the birds of the air. They do not sow or reap, they gather nothing into barns, but your heavenly Father feeds them. Are not you much more valuable than they? Who among you can by worrying add a single cubit to your lifetime? Why are you worried about clothing? See how the lilies of the field grow: they do not work or spin. But I tell you, not even Solomon, in all his splendor, was clothed like one of them. If God so clothes the grass of the field that grows today and is thrown into the fire tomorrow, will he not do much more for you, O you of little faith? Therefore, do not worry and say, 'What are we to eat?' or 'What are we to drink?' or 'What are we to wear?' All these things the pagans seek. Your heavenly Father knows that you need them all. But seek first the kingdom of God and his righteousness, and all these things will be given you besides. And do not worry about tomorrow, for tomorrow will take care of itself. Sufficient for a day is its own evil."*

As there are two masters—money and God—between whom one must choose, as Jesus has just reminded us, so there are two cities: the city of the world and the city of God. These two cities scarcely resemble each other. Their aims are mutually incompatible. The norms of right conduct and the conditions for success differ completely between the two cities.

The service of this world demands an active and continual vigilance: are not the children of this world more clever than the children of light (Luke 16:18)? This world requires competence, street savvy and *savoir faire*, a good dose of diplomacy and tenacity at once: all indispensable qualities for politicians and businesspeople who have a legitimate ambition to serve their country. Their anxieties are those of the moment; their lives go by at a fast clip, and, as the man on the street will readily concede, it's truly a dog's life.

How different is the way of life for believers, for the servants of the kingdom of God. They will have no anxiety for the morrow, says Jesus, nor for food, nor for clothing. They neither sow nor reap, and they do not accumulate reserves in a barn. They abandon themselves in trust. There is another who knows, who takes care, who is always at work.

Therein lies the difference between those who realize themselves in the service of this world and those who gently let themselves be brought to fulfillment by God in their service of his kingdom. The work is different in the two cities: a human work in the first case, the divine work in the latter case. And the power that is deployed is incomparable from one case to the other. On one side, a human dynamic; on the other, the dynamism of God himself, his Holy Spirit.

From this also derive fundamentally different, even mutually exclusive, methods and strategies. In politics, the Gospel is scarcely capable of a literal application, which would lead the politician to certain failure. But likewise in the kingdom of God, or in the church, the boldest political strategies here below would be just as much condemned to futility. They would open the door to a terrible illusion. They would even impede God's activity. Yet God can accomplish more, infinitely more, than this power of action that we provide for him by our strategies, people of little faith that we are. For it is principally he himself who directs his church through the vicissitudes of this world, who fixes its objectives, who chooses its ministers and who endows them with the all-powerful strength of his Spirit: "Do not be so anxious for these things, as the pagans are. Your heavenly Father knows what you need."

In service to the kingdom, Christians' fundamental attitude is to be serenely grounded in the all-powerful love of their Father, like a child. For it is necessary to be a child if one is to enter, and succeed in, the kingdom (Luke 18:17). It is God who calls, he who leads, he who will guide everything to its fulfillment. . . .

And even beyond that. For the heavenly Father has his feet on the ground more than anyone else, if one can speak thus. For those who abandon themselves to him in faith, God will take care not only that they succeed in the kingdom, but will ensure the provision of all that they need in this world, and even of what is additional and gratuitous: "Look at the lilies of the field. . . . Even Solomon in all his splendor was not clothed as one of them. Therefore, seek first the kingdom of God and his righteousness, and all these things will be given you besides."

## Ninth Sunday of Ordinary Time

Matthew 7:21-27

*When the disciples had gathered around Jesus on the mountain, he said to them, "Not everyone who says to me, 'Lord! Lord!' will enter the kingdom of heaven, but only those who do the will of my Father in heaven. On that day, many will say to me, 'Lord, Lord, did we not prophesy in your name? Did we not do mighty deeds in your name?' Then I will declare to them, 'I never knew you. Depart from me, you evildoers!'*

*"Everyone who listens to my words and puts them into practice may be likened to a wise man who built his house on rock. The rain fell, the flood came, and the wind blew and buffeted the house. But it did not fall, for it had been built on rock.*

*"And everyone who hears my words and does not act on them is like a foolish man who built his house on sand. The rain fell, the flood came, and the wind blew and shook the house—and the house fell, and its collapse was total."*

From time to time, Jesus lays down explicit conditions for belonging to the new kingdom. By what indication can those who belong to it be recognized? In today's gospel, Jesus begins by putting us on guard. Illusion in this domain is possible, even frequent. There could be deceptive, external conformity. One could actualize a number of qualities of the kingdom without really belonging to it. Therefore, discernment is required.

First, the tree is not appreciated for its beautiful appeal, or for its foliage, or for its flowers, but rather for its fruit: "By their fruits you will know them." Do people pick grapes from thorns? Or figs from thistles? But what sort of fruits are we discussing here? It is here that the rules of spiritual discernment prove delicate in their exercise. There will be, for example, prophets who prove to be false prophets. Not because their actions fail to have their effect upon others. Quite the contrary! They have indeed prophesied in the name of Jesus; in his name they have cast out demons; they have even worked miracles. In what they have been able to do, there is found testimony to the presence of the kingdom: "If I cast out demons, then the kingdom of God has come among you" (Luke 11:20), Jesus had said. Yet nevertheless, on the last day, Jesus will not recognize them, but will solemnly deny them: "I never knew you" (Matt 25:20).

If the efficacy of our external activity is not a sure mark of the kingdom, could we rest assured in a certain type of relationship with Jesus? But here again, illusion is possible: "It is not everyone who says to me, 'Lord! Lord!' who will enter the kingdom of heaven." Yet to say "Lord" to Jesus is surely to give him the name of God, to confess his divinity. An act of faith, but also an act of prayer. But the fervor or the length of our prayers does not yet constitute a decisive criterion of belonging to the kingdom. Some were condemned by Jesus for their long prayers babbled to gain everyone's attention (Matt 6:7): "It is not everyone who says to me, 'Lord, Lord!' who will enter the kingdom of heaven, but only those who do the will of my Father" (Matt 7:21).

The will of the Father—what does that mean? In the religious parlance to which our ancestors were accustomed, the will of God often seemed like something arbitrary, looming like a menace or suspended over our heads like a sort of sword of Damocles or, at any rate, something constraining. Yet this conception is foreign to the Bible, in which the will of God appears above all as God's good pleasure, at once extraordinarily gentle and powerful, his great desire, his love, his joy from which the whole universe gushes forth.

This will is fully revealed in his Son Jesus as what is most paternal and tender in God, also as what is most delightfully nourishing, since Jesus makes of it his only food (John 4:34). It continues to reveal itself in all those who, like Jesus, are born of this will and this love of God. So for us to do God's will is to go back to our origins, to identify ourselves with the best thing that we possess; it is to remain open to this all-powerful love, to be ceaselessly permeable to it, to let our hearts be impregnated with it, and, finally, to show its traces in all our actions. Far from being ruled by the arbitrary, or weighing us down from the outside, this will is nothing else but a wellspring of love in our innermost depths, God's own gentle joy, his tender design that we embrace patiently, little by little.

Only those who have really known God's love can fulfill his will in all gentleness, without colliding into others or doing violence to themselves. They identify themselves with this will, which is nothing but an immense love. They are gentle and patient. They are merciful after the likeness of the Father, who is merciful (Luke 6:36), whose traits they bear in their hearts and on their faces. And the fruits that they produce, that allow them to judge the tree reliably, are the very fruits of the Spirit: "charity, joy, peace, magnanimity, helpfulness, kindness, faithfulness, mildness" (Gal 5:22), the image of God reflected among us.

# Tenth Sunday of Ordinary Time

## Matthew 9:9-13

*As Jesus went out from Capernaum, he saw a tax collector named Matthew, who was sitting at the customs post, and he said to him, "Follow me!" And he got up and followed him.*

*While Jesus was reclining at table in the house, behold, many tax collectors and sinners came to eat with him and his disciples. Seeing this, the Pharisees said to his disciples, "Why does your master eat with tax collectors and sinners?" On hearing this, Jesus said to them, "Those who are well do not need a physician, but the sick do. Go learn the meaning of these words: 'I desire mercy, not sacrifice.' I did not come to call the righteous, but sinners."*

Jesus does not want sacrifices from human beings, he warns us, for he came not for the righteous but for sinners. What does he mean by that?

The righteous one who offers a sacrifice to God supposes that he thus renounces something for God's sake. He hopes thereby to be made acceptable to him, to sway him, to gain some merit in his eyes. Already in the Old Testament, however, God reproaches such a person for thus deluding himself. These sacrifices are merely tolerated. In the end, they are only a burden to the God who neither eats the flesh of bulls nor drinks the blood of goats.

Such righteous people likewise fail to find favor with Jesus. He very quickly intuits that they basically feel no need of him. They consider themselves to be in good health. Are their lives not in order, precisely in view of their sacrifices? Why would they open themselves to something else, for example, to the love that Jesus came to bring? In reality, Jesus did not come for those who think themselves in order, but for those who have need of mercy. There was no other path by which Jesus could reach us. He does not meet us in our strength, but in our weakness, not in our virtues, but in our sin.

This is the paradox of Jesus, impossible to bypass. A complete reversal of values, which makes it forever impossible to transcribe the Gospel into any humanistic morality, however right-thinking it may be. A reversal that, moreover, grasps each of us in our very depths and corners us into a conversion that is yet scarcely glimpsed. For we too vacillate between these two faces, that of the righteous and that of the sinner—two faces that are both ours besides.

Our righteous face is the one that we display on the outside, even without doing anything explicit whatsoever, a face that we are constantly improving in conformity with the criteria of holiness and of good and due form. Thanks to this face, we manage easily to deceive ourselves without, for all that, fooling the most perspicacious of our brothers and sisters. Above all, we would like to interpose it between ourselves and God, in order to hide ourselves, if it were possible, from his mercy. Our efforts at perfection constitute a subtle game—but one that is so common and so deceptive!

Then there is another face, that of the sinner, hardly pleasing to us and that we perhaps don't even know. In any case, it is one that we don't want to look at squarely and that, therefore, is often compulsively turned away, concealed behind shame. And yet it is chiefly the sinner in us that Jesus wants to unveil, upon whom rests the tenderness of his gaze and the love that alone can save. This sinner in us is located at a more secret depth than that level where all the sins that we have been able to commit, or those we have perhaps not even committed, can be met. It matters little, for there exists within us a still more radical, original, and often more fatal weakness. It lies in our ability to hide from love by eventually taking refuge in sacrifices, in the possibility of withholding ourselves from God's tenderness by counting on our works and by pretending to march alone, whereas only the support of God's mercy can hold us upright.

It is down to this very depth within us that Jesus would penetrate. The absolution of an impressive list of (possibly) committed sins does not suffice for him. He wants rather to take hold of our most fundamental weakness. This is why he is wary of sacrifices that could disguise this weakness, but he waits for the humble love that is not ashamed to disclose it and, in so disclosing it, to expose it to healing.

We must learn to content ourselves with this weakness in order to abide with delight in mercy. Every claim to perfection is superfluous here, even every ideal sanctity is out of place, and to display the face of the righteous would be to wear a mask that keeps us at a distance from Jesus, who prefers to sit at the table of sinners.

## Eleventh Sunday of Ordinary Time

### Matthew 9:36–10:8

*When he saw the vast crowd, Jesus was moved to pity, for they were troubled and abandoned like sheep without a shepherd. He then said to his disciples, "The harvest is abundant, but the laborers are few. Ask, therefore, that the master of the harvest send laborers into his harvest." Then Jesus called his twelve disciples and gave them power to cast out evil spirits and to heal every disease and illness. These are the names of the twelve apostles: first, Simon, called Peter, and his brother Andrew; James, son of Zebedee, and his brother John; Philip and Bartholomew; Thomas and Matthew the tax collector; James, son of Alphaeus, and Thaddeus; Simon the Zealot and Judas Iscariot, who betrayed him. Jesus sent these twelve out with the following instructions: "Do not go into pagan territory or enter a Samaritan town. Go, rather, to the lost sheep of the house of Israel. As you go along, proclaim that the kingdom of heaven is at hand. Cure the sick, raise the dead, cleanse lepers, drive out demons. Without charge, you have received; without charge, you are to give."*

The sight before Jesus' eyes moves him profoundly. Jesus has compassion for these worn out and dejected people seeking relief from the malnutrition that overwhelms them, like abandoned sheep without a shepherd. In his time, as today, the harvest is abundant but the laborers are few.

What is to be done? One might have expected Jesus to hasten to enlist helpers, to inspire generosity or engender "vocations," as we say nowadays. But Jesus contents himself with calling for prayer: "Pray, therefore, that the master of the harvest may send laborers into his harvest."

Indeed, even Jesus will not take the initiative in this domain. Everything derives solely from his Father. He can only do what he sees his Father doing (John 5:19). It is the Father who calls, the Father who sends, albeit through his Son.

The twelve disciples whom Jesus called in a special way had no need to propose themselves. They heard their names in his mouth, and they went forth, not knowing why. Besides, they didn't possess what was necessary to exercise the ministry that Jesus was to confer upon them. No one could have possessed it. They must receive entirely from Jesus what they will need to accomplish their work at the harvest: "He gave them power," says the Gospel, "to cast out evil spirits and to heal every disease and illness."

These powers perpetuate those of Jesus. They are signs that the kingdom is truly here and that the mission can begin. But whether it concerns the powers or the mission, everything is received, nothing can be claimed as one's own: the disciples cannot glorify themselves thereby, or derive any advantage therefrom, whether material or spiritual. In the kingdom of Jesus, all is gratuitous, a gift received with astonishment and thanksgiving and shared likewise with others. Jesus insists on this in a brief saying that well expresses the essence of every mission received from him: "Without charge, you have received; without charge, you are to give."

To receive gratuitously: one might think that this is something easy and rewarding, to possess a treasure without having had to pay any price for it. That might be the case for kingdoms here below, but not in the kingdom that Jesus comes to announce. With him, everything is different. It is true that we receive from him, and abundantly. But there is nothing else to do, in the sense that we have strictly nothing to bring. It is also true that the gifts of Jesus enrich us beyond all for which we could hope. But they strip us bare as well, they impoverish us, they reveal the extent to which we are miserable and naked and that we owe everything to him.

To receive freely, in this world, is to become an owner, to be in a position to sell what one has received, preferably at a good price. To receive the gifts of Jesus, on the contrary, is never to own them, never to be able to attribute them to oneself, and still less to make a profit from them. They are, in addition, not meant for us alone, but are given that they may be passed on in turn to all the brothers and sisters in Christ: "Without charge, you have received; without charge, you are to give."

Such is the dynamic of the kingdom: it is gratuitousness, exactly as God is gratuitous. And whoever would break with this dynamic of gratuitousness to secure his own advantage has already abandoned the mission. He has nullified God's gift by rendering it inoperative. He has given proof that the word that he claims to announce is not the word of God, but a tainted word fabricated by himself in response to his own needs.

On the other hand, those who do not break with the gratuitousness of the gift, who agree to remain entirely transparent to the marvels of God, will attract, on their part, an ever-new gratuitousness. Whoever gives gratuitously will receive still more, always also gratuitously, and the marvels of God will be before her steps.

# Twelfth Sunday of Ordinary Time

## Matthew 10:26-33

*Jesus said to the twelve apostles, "Have no fear of human beings; all that is hidden will be revealed, all that is secret will be made known. What I say to you in the darkness, speak in the light; what you hear whispered in your ear, proclaim from the housetops. And do not fear those who kill the body but cannot kill the soul; fear rather the one who can destroy both soul and body in Gehenna. Are not two sparrows sold for a small coin? Yet not one of them falls to the ground without your Father's consent. As for you, even all the hairs of your head have been counted. Therefore, do not be afraid: you are worth more than all the sparrows in the world. Whoever acknowledges me before others, I will acknowledge before my heavenly Father. But whoever denies me before others, I will also deny before my heavenly Father.*

Have no fear! Do not be afraid of human beings! As it happened to Jesus, so too will it happen to his disciple that, one day, he will be confronted by human beings. He will find himself accused, threatened. In a violent manner by some, in a more subtle fashion by others, but more piercingly for all that! To take the part of Jesus in the heart of our world is always to expose oneself to risk; it is to agree to live dangerously.

This risk is not always apparent. In certain epochs, in fact, faith in Jesus can seem to be identified with the society to such a point that the dangers instead confront those who do not share the faith. It then becomes dangerous not to be a Christian. The threat has changed sides.

But has the true faith also changed sides? This is not the normal situation of the Christian here below, for Jesus tells his disciples that they should not be surprised if the world hates them. A faith transformed into an insurance policy against "all risks" concerning the future, even concerning the life beyond, would be a tainted faith, emptied of its substance.

That is why true faith always includes not only a serious element of obscurity and doubt but also, more or less consciously, feelings of unease and fear. Fear in the face of a world that does not take the believer seriously, inordinate desire for human approval before people who mock Christians, who reject and exclude them, and, worse still, who hurt or kill them. Fear awaits every believer. It even forms part of the faith of each one by bearing witness to its authenticity. For a faith that experiences fear down to the very entrails attests by the fact that it is truly faith in Jesus Christ, in him who was first seized with fear at Gethsemane, before laying down his life for us.

Jesus knows fear well, and he often speaks of it to his disciples: "Do not be afraid," "Fear not" (Luke 7:32). "Do not let your hearts be troubled" (John 14:1-27). "Do not be preoccupied" (Luke 6:25–27). "Do not worry" (Luke 12:11). "Why did you doubt?" (Matt 14:21). "Take courage, I have conquered the world" (John 16:33). This fear in the pit of the stomach throws the disciple of Jesus back into a confidence equal to her fear. What a blessed fear it is that roots one ever deeper in the Father's love.

The image of the sparrows that Jesus uses is suggestive. They are so little valued, yet "not one of them falls to the ground without your Father's consent. . . . Therefore, do not be afraid: you are worth more than all the sparrows in the world." The Father's love pursues even the humblest of his creatures, even down to these sparrows small enough to be nestled in one's hand. Jesus seems to have recalled this image when, in John's gospel, he tells us that we belong to his Father and that no one can snatch us from his hand. We are held thus, like sparrows nestled in the palm of our Father's hand.

The Father takes care even of what is most fragile and most ephemeral in our bodies: our hair, of which we lose a certain amount every day. It doesn't matter—not one of our hairs falls to the ground, Jesus assures us, without the Father knowing and willing it: "As for you, even all the hairs of your head have been counted."

Sometimes it can be good to feel our fears, to feel at the same time the extent to which they force us to turn to God; or to feel trouble and discouragement, so that we can experience the truth that only the peace that Jesus can give us will suffice to bring us peace; or to feel day after day the humiliating sting of our repeated failures, that we might no longer place our confidence in anything but the power of God alone; or to find oneself a hopeless sinner, that one might finally cast oneself upon his love that is mercy. "Do not be afraid! The Father knows what you need!"

## Thirteenth Sunday of Ordinary Time

Matthew 10:37-42

*Jesus said to the twelve apostles, "Whoever loves father or mother more than me is not worthy of me; whoever loves son or daughter more than me is not worthy of me; whoever does not take up his cross and follow me is not worthy of me. Whoever seeks to save his life will lose it, but whoever loses his life for my sake will keep it.*

*"Whoever receives you, receives me. And whoever receives me, receives the one who sent me. Whoever receives a prophet because he is a prophet will receive a prophet's reward. Whoever receives a righteous man will receive a righteous man's reward. And whoever gives even a cup of cold water to one of these little ones because he is a disciple . . . amen, I say to you, he will surely not lose his reward."*

Without Jesus, the destiny of humanity here below would be without issue. Ever since God became man and assumed our entire destiny even to the point of death and resurrection, every human existence that pretends not to know Jesus ends in an impasse. In fact, Jesus entered upon the paths of human life to such an extent that he obstructed one of them—definitively—by his death, and at the same time he opened another one—the only one that can henceforth lead anywhere—by his resurrection.

Jesus himself affirmed this: he is henceforward the unique way, outside of which no one can any longer reach the goal: "No one comes to the Father except through me" (John 14:6). He is also the gate, the only gate, through which one must pass to enter into the kingdom (John 10:7-9).

Sooner or later, it will be important to commit oneself to this unique way and to pass through this one gate. But, as Jesus warns us, this gate is narrow and restrictive. Many, perhaps the greater number of people, hesitate for a long time and choose the wrong gate, committed as they are to a wide and easy path that will reveal itself to be a bad one, as they will all too soon experience for themselves. This path ends in a cul-de-sac.

One day, whether we will it or not, whether we have prepared ourselves by carefully marking out the trails, or whether we have become a bit thoughtless in the course of our journey, we will have to pass by Jesus. Or, rather, it is he who discreetly, almost slyly—if the word can have a positive sense—has already introduced himself into our way, there especially where obstacles were multiplying and the route was becoming a bit tortuous. He has anticipated us on our own ground and now waits for us to turn to him. He is the inescapable one.

At the beginning, and for a rather long time, we do not recognize him. Without our knowing it, however, he had already gained a foothold in our life. By small signs, scarcely blinking, he makes us understand that the hour has come for us to abandon a path that leads nowhere, so that we might follow him alone and his path, which he tells us is narrow. Suddenly, we become aware that he is identified with our most intimate desires, that he has woven his way into our heart. Our most audacious plans, our legitimate ambitions, our most cherished affections—none of it escapes him any longer. Here he is, mixed up with our secret life. He has taken root in our unconscious. Impossible from now on to go forward, except by leaving behind the earlier path that was broad and easy. Once we had to pass by others first—our parents, our friends, our brothers and sisters—in order to reach Jesus. Today, we must first pass by Jesus before we reach others. And, to pass by him, we must leave the others before rediscovering them in him: "Whoever loves father and mother more than me is not worthy of me; whoever loves son or daughter more than me is not worthy of me" (Matt 10:37).

Paradox of the way of Jesus: those who have been most indispensable to our life and growth—father and mother—and those to whom we have been most indispensable—sons and daughters—we must leave, to be able to follow Jesus to the end. This is the crucial point of the way, the place where it becomes the most restrictive, where it becomes a way of the cross: "Whoever does not take up his cross and follow me is not worthy of me" (Luke 14:27).

Of this moment that we fear—and rightly so, since Jesus feared it before us, even with a fear and a sorrow unto death (Matt 26:38)—of this moment we know only two things. First, that we will no longer have anything before us but Jesus alone, Jesus who invites us. Then, that this will be the blessed moment when our path will finally reach its goal, when the old life will empty out into resurrection and new life: "Whoever seeks to save his life will lose it; whoever loses his life for my sake will save it" (Matt 10:39).

# Fourteenth Sunday of Ordinary Time

## Matthew 11:25-30

*At that time, Jesus opened his mouth and said, "I give you praise, Father, Lord of heaven and earth. For what you have hidden from the wise and the learned, you have revealed to little ones. Yes, Father, for that has been your gracious will. All things have been handed over to me by my Father. No one knows the Son except the Father, and no one knows the Father except the Son and anyone to whom the Son wishes to reveal him.*

*"Come to me, all you who labor and are burdened, and I will give you rest. Take my yoke upon you, and learn from me, for I am meek and humble of heart, and you will find rest for your souls. For my yoke is easy and my burden is light."*

"The wise and the learned": these are two qualifiers that hold nothing dishonorable for people of our time. Quite the contrary: wisdom is a virtue, and knowledge is a quality that one has a right to seek. Jesus, for his part, does not condemn them in any way. He simply notes that it is not to those with such endowments that his Father reveals the secrets of his kingdom. And not only has he not revealed these secrets to such persons, but he has even hidden the mysteries from them, that they might not know them.

Why, then, have the wise and the learned been left out? Jesus does not tell us explicitly. He nevertheless insists that this sorting depends entirely on the sovereign freedom of the Father's will: "Yes, Father, for that has been your gracious will." If there is a preference, it is because the Father willed it so. No accident, no necessity, but a free choice bordering on the arbitrary.

But just bordering on it. For the Father does not find his joy in separating people out or hiding things from them. If he hides from some, it is so as to have the joy of revealing to others. For the Father has preferences, but his preferences do not follow the pattern of human preferences. They are surprising. If there is something arbitrary about them, it pertains to the arbitrariness of love. The first reflex of his love does not move towards the wise and the learned, toward those who know and who are able, but toward the little ones, says Jesus.

Who are these little ones? In one of his epistles, Saint Paul elaborates on this theme of the Father's preference for the little ones and gives us a description of them. They are the ones who have no status in the eyes of the world, those who are not worth anything, who are nothing or who, quite simply, in the eyes of others, do not even exist (1 Cor 1:27-28). Is it a matter of cultural or material poverty? Maybe. Spiritual poverty? Certainly. God has preferred these "nobodies," Paul explains, so that no human beings may glorify themselves before God. Chosen because they do not know, and because they know that they don't know; because they are not able to do anything, not even to resist God, so disarmed are they before his choice and before his grace.

It was essential, indeed, to be quite little so as not to balk at the revelation that God wanted to make, a revelation so surprising that it could only have calcified the refusal of those who considered themselves knowledgeable, our "wise and learned." A revelation of the Father and of the Son and of the extraordinary communion of love that binds them together in the Spirit. But can one know the Father, unless one finds oneself at least a little in the place of the Son? And how can one know the Son, unless one already knows the Father? Jesus proclaims it solemnly: "No one knows the Father except the Son and anyone to whom the Son wishes to reveal him."

In the kingdom of Jesus, the choice of being either on the side of the wise or on the side of the little ones presents itself to us continually, and it is always delicate to put it into effect. To take the part of the poor and plead their cause is still relatively easy, much easier than one day obtaining a place at their side before God, who is just as poor as they or even poorer. It is much more comfortable to criticize the learned and intellectuals in the church than one day to have to admit to no longer knowing anything in the face of God's mystery. For what is demanded of us—or, rather, offered to us—is something totally different, beyond all knowledge, beyond all charitable activity. It is the one thing necessary, about which we can say only that we have not yet received it and that we daily desire and request it, madly. The one thing necessary that Jesus alone can teach us, via contact with him: "Learn from me that I am meek and humble of heart, and you will find rest for your souls" (Matt 11:29). And, through the rest and peace of your heart, thousands around you will be saved.

# Fifteenth Sunday of Ordinary Time

## Matthew 13:1-23

*On that day, Jesus left the house and sat down on the shore of the lake. A great crowd gathered around him, so that he got into a boat and sat down, while the crowd remained on the shore. He spoke to them at length in parables: "A sower went out to sow. And as he sowed, some seed fell on the path, and the birds came and ate it up. Some seed fell on rocky ground, where the soil was not deep. It sprouted at once because of the little soil, but when the sun rose it was scorched, and it withered for lack of roots. Some seed fell among thorns, and the thorns grew up and choked it. And some seed fell on good soil, where it sprouted and bore fruit, now a hundredfold, now sixtyfold, now thirtyfold. Whoever has ears ought to hear."*

*The disciples approached Jesus and asked him, "Why do you speak to them in parables?" He said in reply, "Because the knowledge of the mysteries of the kingdom of heaven is given to you, but to them it has not been given. To the one who has, more will be given. But from the one who has not, even what he has will be taken away. If I speak to them in parables, it is so that looking, they may not see, and listening, they may not hear or understand. Thus is fulfilled in them the prophecy of Isaiah that says, 'However much you listen, you will not understand. However much you look, you will not see. Weighed down is the heart of this people:*

*they have stopped up their ears, they have closed their eyes, so that their eyes may not see, their ears may not hear, nor their hearts understand, lest they be converted and I heal them!'*

*"But blessed are your eyes because they see! Blessed are your ears because they hear! Amen, I say to you, many prophets and righteous people longed to see what you see and did not see it, to hear what you hear and did not hear it.*

*"Hear, therefore, the meaning of the parable of the sower. When someone hears the word of the kingdom without understanding, the Evil One comes and takes away what was sown in his heart. This is the seed sown on the path.*

*"The seed sown on rocky soil, this is the one who hears the word and receives it at once with joy, but he has no root and lasts only for a time; as soon as some affliction or persecution comes because of the word, he immediately falls away.*

*"The seed sown among thorns, this is the one who hears the word, but worldly anxiety and the lure of riches choke the word so that it bears no fruit.*

*"But the seed sown on good soil, this is the one who hears the word with understanding and bears fruit, now a hundredfold, now sixtyfold, now thirtyfold."*

The word of God contains an irresistible strength. It never falls short of its goal or returns to God without having accomplished its mission. That is the principal teaching of the readings that we have just heard.

Indeed, the word is pregnant with life, the very life of God: a life as vigorous as that of the seed that already bears mysteriously within itself the grown tree and the ripe fruit. Ordinarily, it suffices to let nature take its course, to unfold its potentialities. Every sowing, however meager it may be, will one day germinate, bringing forth first the blade, then the stem, then a trunk, and finally flowers and fruits, everything in its time, imperturbably. No effort need be added from without, as Jesus himself says one day (Matt 6:27). It is enough for someone to cast the seed upon the ground, and, afterward, he can rest and sleep (Mark 4:27). Of itself, the seed sprouts and grows and produces fruit. So it is also with the all-powerful life of God that dwells within the least of his words that the Bible and the liturgy sow unceasingly in our hearts.

This first affirmation seems to be called into question, however, or at least brought to completion, by a second one that constitutes precisely the point of the parable of the sower that we have just heard. For this life of God, so vigorous, can be rendered ineffectual by inadvertence—by inadvertence, indeed, by unreadiness, by distraction on the part of the one who should be there to welcome it. A frightful power, or rather powerlessness, of the human being to whom God takes the risk of exposing himself. The wonders that he wanted to accomplish by means of his Word can be annulled, brought to nothing by human inattention. And this same human being who had previously been destined, and specially called, and chosen by God to be his instrument, can no longer be anything but the obstacle that holds God in check and cuts short the progress of the miracle.

For God decided once and for all to respect human freedom, not to force any miracle, but to sow his Word, even at a pure loss in soil that is not loose and fertile.

Every sowing, in fact, if it is to germinate and grow, requires loose soil, in which it will be able to take the time to die and rise into new life for the next harvest. Neither the dirt of the well-trodden path, nor the rocky soil, nor the fallow soil infested with thistles and weeds can render this service. The same holds true for the word of life that the divine sower ardently desires to entrust to us. In a hard soil made stony and hard by worries and activities, encumbered by riches, restless with rivalries and ambitions, the seed of God finds itself terribly confined: it is condemned to vegetate sadly and never really to develop. It is constantly threatened with suffocation. It is not the sower who is to blame—every day, he goes out to sow generously, royally—but the earth that is not ready and fit to give a chance to the divine life.

Once again, we find here a fearsome power, in one sense or the other: power to give free rein to the might of God through his Word and to become in the midst of the church a source of life and of miracles, or indeed to be able to stop dead the flow of God's wonders. In the latter case—more often than not, alas!—it is neither by malice nor by cowardice, but by simple inattention, whereas it would have sufficed to offer God an attentive and unencumbered heart, a heart truly in love with the Word, that through it God might bring forth abundant fruit, even thirty or sixty or a hundredfold.

# Sixteenth Sunday of Ordinary Time

## Matthew 13:24-43

*He proposed another parable to them: "The kingdom of heaven may be likened to a mustard seed that a man planted in a field. It is the smallest of all seeds, but, when fully grown, it is the largest of plants and becomes a tree, and the birds of the air come and nest in its branches."*

*He told them another parable: "The kingdom of heaven is like leaven that a woman took and mixed with three measures of flour, until the whole batch was leavened."*

*In all this, Jesus spoke to the crowd in parables, and without parables he said nothing to them, thus fulfilling the word of the prophet: "I will open my mouth in parables and reveal things hidden from the foundation of the world."*

*Then, leaving the crowd, he went into the house. His disciples approached and said to him, "Explain to us clearly the parable of the darnel in the field." He said in reply, "The sower of good seed is the Son of Man; the field is the world; the good seed, these are the children of the kingdom; the darnel, these are the children of the Evil One; the enemy who sows them is the devil, the harvest is the end of the world, and the harvesters are angels. Just as darnel is removed and thrown into the fire, so shall it be at the end of the world. The Son of Man will send his angels, and they will remove from his kingdom all those who cause others to sin and all evildoers and will throw them into the fire, where there will be wailing and gnashing of teeth. But the righteous will shine like the sun in the kingdom of their Father.*

*"Whoever has ears ought to hear."*

The kingdom of God is never without darnel. The good seed and the weeds grow there side by side. Like the servants in the parable, it is often difficult for us to accept this. We would like a Bride of Christ who is from the start without wrinkle or stain (Eph 5:27). And we grow discouraged. We resent those who are responsible. We make accusations, we seek an urgent intervention. Sometimes, someone will throw in the towel and completely turn his back on the kingdom.

It is true of the church, which we would like to be above all suspicion, whereas good and evil cohabit there strangely and sometimes, at least in our eyes, scandalously. A scandal all the more painful to endure, because more humiliating, when we perceive that the good seed and the darnel mingle not only outside of us, but even in the depths of our own heart. There too, the two grow together cheerfully. Our heart, every day sown with the Word of God and with his grace, nevertheless presents obvious traces of the darnel. And even if we are disposed to hasten to extirpate the darnel from another's field, how should we go about uprooting it from our own heart?

The problem is aggravated by the fact that we are ourselves incapable of clearly distinguishing between what grows out of the good seed and what derives from the darnel. That is why Jesus cautions those who would attack the darnel immediately, as the two plants are so difficult to separate before the end of time, before the kingdom of Jesus has borne all its fruit. Today there remains too great a risk of confusing the two and pulling up the good grain in the attempt to get rid of the darnel.

We are, in fact, visually impaired where the human heart is concerned, especially our own heart. There are virtues that are only seeming virtues and that ably conceal vices. And there are equally merely apparent defects that unjustly hide what is at a deeper level genuine virtue. It is easy to deceive others; it is still easier to be mistaken oneself, often without knowing it and with the best of intentions.

It is for this reason that Jesus prescribes the only possible tactic—"Let them grow together until the harvest"—when his angels will be charged with infallibly separating the good and the evil.

"Let the two grow together": this instruction does not simplify things, does not make our situation in the kingdom easier. Rather, it makes our place in the kingdom uncomfortable. It demands from us much patience, as well as a lot of humility, to accept that the field of the church, or that of our community, or the field of our own heart should present itself so infested, so disfigured by evil, even if we know that such is the normal condition of the kingdom of God today.

But there is something still more uncomfortable. The good seed and the darnel do not get along together. On the contrary, they are pitted against each other in a struggle that is all the more hidden as we remain continually disabled in our attempts to identify them correctly. Thus at every hour the darnel threatens the good seed, and the good seed, in turn, unceasingly threatens the darnel. One of the two could always choke off the other, our heart being the battleground where they confront each other without respite.

The outcome of this confrontation is not uncertain, however. Far from it!—if only we devote ourselves to it patiently and humbly, in faith. For the sowing of the kingdom will one day prove more powerful, and irresistibly so. But if it is at first the smallest and most insignificant, no greater than a mustard seed that is the smallest of seeds, it will one day produce a fruit that will surpass in height the largest of trees, as Jesus has just assured us. Even if most of the time it is, so to speak, invisible, buried like leaven in the dough, it is called one day to raise up the entire world (Matt 13:33). It is enough for us to trust in the Word of God and in his omnipotence that dwells therein (Mark 4:27).

# Seventeenth Sunday of Ordinary Time

## Matthew 13:44-52

*Jesus told these parables to the crowd: "The kingdom of heaven is like a treasure hidden in a field that a man discovers and hides again. And out of joy, he goes and sells all that he has and buys that field. Or, again, the kingdom of heaven is like a merchant in search of fine pearls. When he finds a pearl of great price, he goes and sells everything he has and buys that pearl.*

*"Again, the kingdom of heaven is like a net that is cast into the sea where it collects all kinds of fish. When it is full, they draw it ashore, sit down, and fill buckets with what is good, while what is bad they throw away. Thus will it be at the end of the age: the angels will come and separate the wicked from the righteous and will throw them into the fiery furnace, where there will be wailing and grinding of teeth.*

*"Have you understood all this?"—"Yes," they replied. Then Jesus said, "Then every scribe in the kingdom of heaven will be like the head of a household who brings from his storeroom both the new and the old."*

To sell all that one has to gain the kingdom: at first sight, this is an exorbitant demand. Who would want to pay such a price, to be bled so dry?

The price only seems so exorbitant in the eyes of those who do not yet know the treasure. They are probably numerous, and we are perhaps among them, since Jesus says explicitly that this treasure is normally hidden. It lies buried in a certain field, and there may be innumerable passersby who roam this field without ever suspecting the fortune that lies beneath their feet. Until, one day, someone comes upon the treasure and discovers it at a moment of grace.

Blessed discovery and distinguished privilege! Why this person, and not someone else? The evangelist does not answer this question any more than he makes any mention of the efforts that the fortunate one must have expended before being crowned with this success. On the contrary, it seems to be a case of gratuitous surprise, a divine gift of sheer grace. God chooses whom he will. Today as well, the treasure of the kingdom is hidden, and no human effort can unearth it. Only the person whose eyes the Lord opens suddenly will discover it.

But then, what rapture, what crashing, overwhelming joy, and what desire to acquire the treasure at once, without delay and at any price! A price that will be, at any rate, negligible in comparison to the anticipated delight: "Out of joy, he goes and sells all that he has and buys that field." Is it madness? Certainly, for the one has not yet made this discovery. But for the one who is in on the secret and knows the treasure, it is wisdom.

The important thing is to have made the discovery and to let oneself be drawn by its allure, to overflow with the joy of it. God could raise the price, but what does it matter? So great a joy makes all costs negligible. No price would be too high, none would cause us to renounce the treasure. On the contrary, whoever has discovered the treasure and, at the same time, his mad yearning to acquire it, is ready to renounce every other joy for this one, a greater joy that brushes aside every other one.

Once again, what is important here is the joy, and that such a great renunciation be effectively preceded by such a great joy. For renunciation is only healthy and salutary in the measure that it is marked beforehand by such a joy, the joy of discovering the treasure, the joy of the Holy Spirit in the depths of our heart. Without this joy, any renouncement would be a risky enterprise, exposed to many ambiguities. At the extreme, it could extinguish all desire within us, obstruct our interior wellspring, and even suffocate the desire for God, which is precisely the most precious treasure of all but also the one most deeply buried in the field of the heart.

We may have had occasion to act as if the contrary were true, as if renunciation were the condition of a consequent spiritual joy that God would measure out to us by the yardstick of our efforts. The greater the pains endured today, the greater the joy that would issue therefrom. But today's parable reminds us that the order is the reverse. If the joy of God does not precede them, our renunciations will be glum, sad, fruitless; they will be off-putting to others and make the kingdom distasteful to them.

Of course, for us to discover the treasure of our joy, it is in a certain sense necessary for God to take the initiative. But after that, it is up to us. For when God has revealed to us our joy—and he will not fail to do so, one day or another—we often don't dare to believe in it. Or, if we believe in it a little, we don't dare to follow through to the consummation of our joy, to pursue the jubilation of the Holy Spirit wherever it leads us. It is a prodigious adventure that can lead us where we would never have dared hope, and at any price.

# Eighteenth Sunday of Ordinary Time

## Matthew 14:13-21

*Jesus set off in the boat for a desert place by himself. The crowds learned of it and, leaving their villages, followed him on foot. On disembarking and seeing the vast crowd, he was moved with pity for them, and he cured their sick. When evening came, the disciples approached him and said, "This is a deserted place, and the hour is getting late. Therefore, dismiss the crowd, that they may go to the surrounding villages and buy food for themselves." Jesus said to them, "There is no need for them to go away. Give them some food yourselves." But they said to him, "Five loaves and two fish are all we have." Jesus answered, "Bring them here to me." Then he ordered the crowd to recline on the grass. Taking the five loaves and the two fish, and raising his eyes to heaven, he said the blessing, broke the loaves, and gave them to the disciples, who distributed them to the crowds. All ate and were satisfied. And with the leftover fragments, they filled twelve wicker baskets. Those who ate were about five thousand men, not counting women and children.*

Jesus had wished to elude their pursuit. He had gone in a boat to a deserted place. But they were not discouraged by this. They leave the city to follow him into the very wilderness. Without calculation, without forethought, in response to a spontaneous idea or, rather, to the heart's sudden impulse.

Jesus had dazzled them by his word, by his healings, but above all by something basically inexpressible that is proper to human beings in his uniqueness: the profound and irresistible charm of his person, of himself and no one else. From a number of angles, their venture might have seemed a species of madness, like that of those who have fallen in love or are on the verge of doing so, letting themselves be swept off their feet, ready to fall into the trap of what they take to be love.

The confirmation of their thoughtlessness is not long in waiting: at evening's fall, in a place that is indeed isolated, they lack provisions and are hungry. What to do now? The apostles take up this concern and propose a common-sense solution: simply set out on the way again, leave the wilderness to go and replenish supplies in the villages. But can anyone leave the company of Jesus after being so seized with longing for him? Besides, Jesus is of a different view: the solution is not to retrace their steps, for what they need is hidden in the wilderness itself: "There is no need for them to go away," he says in reply; "Give them some food yourselves."

Alas, the disciples' resources are absurdly limited: merely five loaves and two fish. Indeed, when we have followed Jesus to the end, when we find ourselves as if finally caught in his snare, the resources we have at our disposal are always cruelly deficient, incommensurate with the challenge that Jesus proposes. Our reserves run out in no time; in the blink of an eye, they are exhausted.

Then it is that everything can begin. Once we have been taken in Jesus' snare, when we have literally been caught by him, then there is no longer any more than one possible outcome. Not to recoil, not to turn around, not to try to cope by means of our human resources. Snared by Jesus, we can no longer come out of the trap except through Jesus and because of Jesus. There, where we have entered for love of him, a moment arrives when we can no longer either advance or persevere except thanks to that same love. But it is then a love that goes all the way to the end, a love that no snare can restrain within its netting, a love as strong as death that torrents of trials and temptations cannot extinguish. A love that the desert can only cause to dig deeper.

Why? Because once the love of Jesus has really taken hold of us, nothing, absolutely nothing, can any longer separate us from this same love. The apostle Paul recalls this to us in the second reading in the most ardent terms: "Who will separate us from the love of Christ? Will distress? Or anguish? Or persecution? Or hunger? Or nakedness? Or danger? Or the sword? No, for in all this we conquer overwhelmingly because of him who has loved us. For I am utterly convinced that nothing, absolutely nothing can separate us from the love of God in Christ Jesus our Lord."

It is this love that works miracles. It multiplies loaves, it heals the sick, it forgives sins. Love: not so much our own, but rather the confidence that we have dared to place in the love of Jesus, at the center of what seemed to be a trap ready to enclose us. In fact, there is no trap, but only a path still momentarily concealed, an outcome not yet envisaged, that would perhaps have remained forever obstructed if we had not, one day, dazzled by Jesus, consented to follow him to the end, if we had not persevered in expecting everything from him alone. O blessed snare, O delightful path, O extraordinary school of freedom where we let ourselves be caught in this way—but caught by his love!

# Nineteenth Sunday of Ordinary Time

Matthew 14:22-33

*Immediately after feeding the multitude in the wilderness, Jesus made his disciples get into the boat and precede him to the other side, while he dismissed the crowds. After he had dismissed them, he went up on the mountain to pray by himself. When it was evening, he was there alone. The boat, which had already traveled a good distance from the shore, was being pummeled by the waves, for the wind was against it.*

*Toward the end of the night, Jesus came to them, walking on the sea. When they saw him walking on the sea, the disciples were terrified. They were saying, "It's a ghost!" and they cried out in fear. At once, Jesus said to them, "Take courage! It is I. Do not be afraid!" Peter then said to him, "Lord, if it is you, command me to come to you on the water." Jesus said to him, "Come!" Peter got out of the boat and began to walk on the water toward Jesus. But when he saw how strong the wind was, he became frightened, and, beginning to sink, he cried out, "Lord, save me!" Immediately, Jesus reached out his hand, seized him, and said to him, "O you of little faith, why did you doubt?" And when they got back into the boat, the wind died down. Then those in the boat did him homage, saying to him, "Truly, you are the Son of God!"*

Today's Gospel is divided into two panels, each of which depicts a scene with Jesus and his disciples. In the first panel, they are separated; in the second, they come together again in mutual recognition.

In the first act, the disciples are at sea and encountering difficulties. The wind is against them, and the boat is being violently pounded by the waves. Jesus, still on shore, has withdrawn to a mountain by himself to pray. A long moment, it seems, that lasts until the end of the night.

During the day, Jesus is surrounded by people. At night, he meets his Father. Once the light of the sun has faded, another hearth is lit for him, the light that he carries secretly within himself and that he shares with his Father in a scintillating intimacy. Indeed, God is light, and in him there is no darkness (1 John 1:5).

Like Elijah, standing before his cave in the gentle murmur of the breeze, like so many watchers peering into the darkness of the world and of their own hearts, Jesus neither sleeps nor slumbers, he, the guardian of Israel (Ps 120:4). He inhabits the night with all the weight of his vigil. He enjoys an audience with his Father without, for all that, abandoning his disciples.

They too keep vigil, but in struggle and distress. Their confidence is in this Jesus who is praying at a distance and whom they would so much prefer to have with them in the boat. But between them and him there is, at this hour, the impassable distance posed by a tumultuous sea. Distance of their doubting hearts as well. But behold, just before the break of day, Jesus comes to them at the precise moment when, at the end of their rope, they feel an urgent need of him. Everything within them is crying out for Jesus and opening up in readiness to meet him. They are entirely accessible. But in spite of that, they fail to recognize him and take him for a phantom.

When Jesus wants to meet us in the midst of our squalls and our struggles, it sometimes—even rather often—

happens that everything begins with an analogous error. While we are struggling, he, from a distance on the mountain, up above at the right hand of the Father, stands and makes constant intercession for us (Heb 7:25). His presence to us is total, but not immediately perceptible. We do not see him, we do not touch him with the parts of our body. Between himself and us, there is the apparent abyss of our doubts and our afflictions. And when he draws near to us to make known his presence and to allow us to recognize him, our bewilderment redoubles. We feel ourselves more alone than ever, and we are seized with paroxysm of fear.

For Jesus reveals himself to us in a way completely different from what we expected. He does not present himself to the eyes of our flesh but to those of our faith, of our heart—eyes that are barely open, a still-somnolent heart, an ever-vacillating faith. At first glance, Jesus appears to us entirely unreal, improbable, maybe even dangerous. We were expecting him to come in a thunderclap, but here he is in peace and gentleness. We counted on success; he comes with failure. We were looking for glory; he offers lowliness. And if we wish nevertheless to take a chance on this phantom, to accept a personal risk for his sake, we must, like Peter, entrust ourselves to the impossible walk upon the water and even agree to sink into a faith rendered more than improbable.

It is just there that Jesus takes hold of us, at the heart of our lack of faith: "O you of little faith, why did you doubt?" No doubt it was essential that we be engulfed by the waters of despair before we dared to abandon ourselves to Jesus. He is, however, always among us, even in the heart of the storm. All that is required of us is to dare to believe, but he alone can teach us to do so: "I believe, Lord, increase my faith" (Luke 17:5).

# Twentieth Sunday of Ordinary Time

## Matthew 15:21-28

*Jesus withdrew to the region of Tyre and Sidon. A Canaanite woman from that district approached him and cried out, "Have pity on me, Lord, Son of David, for my daughter is tormented by a demon." But he did not answer her one word. The disciples approached him and said, "Give her what she wants, for she keeps crying out and following us!" Jesus said in reply, "I have not been sent except to the lost sheep of the house of Israel." But she drew near and prostrated herself before him, saying, "Lord, help me!" He answered, "It is not right to take the children's bread and throw it to the little dogs." She said in reply, "True, Lord. But even the little dogs eat the scraps that fall from their masters' tables." Jesus responded, "O woman, great is your faith! Let what you have wished be done for you!" And her daughter was healed from that hour.*

A foreign woman, a Canaanean, compels Jesus to cross a border that had been up till then jealously closed. As Israel was the uniquely chosen people, the other nations were, without distinction, simply considered to be pagans, excluded from the salvation that God had promised his people. Jesus himself seems to have held this doctrine before meeting this pagan. Though she lays out her daughter's distress before Jesus' eyes, he appears uncharacteristically unmoved. He lets this woman continue to beseech him without paying her any mind.

When his disciples, having had enough of her noisy supplication, come to him to take up her cause—"give her what she wants, for she keeps crying out and following us!"—Jesus simply refuses, and on a basis that leaves no room for argument, as it touches on the very mission that he has received from his Father: "I have not been sent," he says, "except to the lost sheep of the house of Israel." To speak plainly: this woman is a foreigner. She does not belong to the chosen people. She can claim no right to those wonderful works and miracles that announce the proximity of salvation. These latter are strictly reserved to those whom God has chosen for himself.

This woman had nevertheless attempted to assimilate herself to the Jews by borrowing their vocabulary. In addressing Jesus, she calls him "Lord" and even "Son of David," two titles of immense significance that very few Jews would have been ready to concede to Jesus during his lifetime. To hear her, one would take this Canaanite woman to be already a believer.

Alas! Even this semblance of faith is not enough to shake the firm resolve of Jesus, who remains rooted in his principled stance: this woman is not a Jew, she has no just claim. Who is she, then, to dare steal the bread meant for the children of the race? And Jesus' reply feels truly biting: "It is not right to take the children's bread and throw it to the little dogs."

"Little dog!" A hurtful expression. It comes close to insult and to racism. The woman might have felt cut to the quick, stood up suddenly, turned her back on Jesus and proudly marched off. After all, she would have been in the right, she would have had cause. How could Jesus humiliate this pagan woman to such a degree?

But she does exactly the opposite. In fact, the humiliation that Jesus inflicts on her seems calculated on his part: it is this very thing that will save her. It will open her to a faith so fresh, so guileless, so disarming, that it will end up vanquishing, at once, Jesus' principled resistance. The little dogs? "True, Lord," she replies. "But even the little dogs eat the scraps that fall from their masters' tables." One could hardly be simpler or truer. It is a true stroke of genius on the woman's part, a conjoined trait of humility and of faith. Jesus can resist no longer: "O woman, great is your faith! Let what you have wished be done for you."

A hitherto jealously guarded border has just been crossed by Jesus. A pagan woman has conquered him, led him where he did not want to go. Not because this woman cried out more loudly or obstinately than any other, nor because her distress was more poignant. But only because she consents to take a certain place, not at the table, but under the table, less than the last place: that of the little dog who comes to eat not the bread, but merely the scraps of mercy.

It is by this altogether little door that we, Gentiles that we are, were one day admitted into the church by Jesus. It is through this little door that we may also, at our own little place, hope one day to receive the scraps of mercy. As Saint Paul reminded us at the end of the second reading, these scraps fall for us in view of our poverty because, he says, "God has enclosed all human beings in weakness, and even in sin, that he might have mercy on all" (Rom 11:32).

## Twenty-first Sunday of Ordinary Time

Matthew 16:13-20

*Jesus went to the region of Caesarea Philippi. He asked his disciples, "Who do people say that the Son of Man is?" They said in reply, "Some say John the Baptist, others Elijah, still others Jeremiah or one of the prophets." Jesus said to them, "But you, who do you say that I am?" Simon Peter took this up and said, "You are the Messiah, the Son of the Living God!" Jesus then said to him, "Blessed are you, Simon son of Jonah, for flesh and blood did not reveal this to you, but my heavenly Father. Therefore I declare to you that you are Peter, and upon this rock I will build my church, and the gates of the nether world will not prevail against it. I will give you the key of the kingdom of heaven: whatever you bind on earth shall be bound in heaven; whatever you loose on earth shall be loosed in heaven." Then he commanded his disciples to tell no one that he was the Messiah.*

Jesus' true identity remained long enveloped in mystery, a mystery that Jesus himself cultivated. Even in this Gospel pericope, at the same moment when Peter recognizes him as the Son of the Living God, he gives the command not to repeat this to anyone. Meanwhile, it is a secret, jealously guarded by those closest to him.

Others are not lacking for their own personal ideas about him: could he be John the Baptist? Or Elijah? Or Jeremiah? Or one of the prophets? Everyone offers his own opinion, each more respectable than the previous one. They could thus continue for a long time before they had ever run through all the great figures in the Bible, or even in the whole human race, whom Jesus might distantly resemble. But it would be in vain. Jesus is incomparable: no one, be they ever so accomplished, could ever really compare to him.

For flesh and blood—that is, human beings left to their own lights, however penetrating—are not capable of recognizing Jesus. What is required is another sort of light, coming from elsewhere. Only the Father in person can reveal his own Son, to whom he will and when he will (Matt 11:27). Until the blessed hour of such a revelation, the Jews—even the most perspicacious, the most erudite, the most observant of the Law, even his own disciples who had followed him for months, could do no more than lose themselves in more or less probable conjectures in this regard, all of them equally contestable.

Our present condition with respect to Jesus is hardly any different. His person remains cloaked in mystery. Fascinating to some, repellant to others, the figure of Jesus still lends itself to every imaginable interpretation. And there is no lack of great religious geniuses to whom one is tempted, even today, to compare him, among whom one might wish to enthrone him—as if thus to bestow on him a great honor. Alas! now that his resurrection from the dead has clearly manifested his divine being, Jesus is more incomparable than ever, elusive to creatures, beyond all human comprehension.

Still today, we require another light, coming from elsewhere. Still today, only the Father can draw us to his Son and reveal him to us, according to the good pleasure of his love (John 6:44).

As easily done as said? Far from it! The enigma surrounding Jesus can last a long time, and his secret may appear sealed. Of course, one can learn a lot of things *about* Jesus: a probing and sincere historian may, for instance, succeed in composing a brilliant biography of him, but without ever having received this revelation from the Father. And even after becoming a believer, one could correctly recite all the formulas of faith concerning Jesus; one could even teach them to others as an expert catechist—without ever having had one's heart touched by the Father or inflamed by the Spirit. One could even learn properly all of Jesus' commandments and strive faithfully to conform to them and, for all that, remain a stranger to the Father's revelation and not in the least touched by it.

That's because flesh and blood are never sufficient for this, nor a correct catechism, nor a moral life beyond reproach. Something more is needed, indeed the essential thing, that no human beings however just, that no disciples however close to Jesus can ever bestow on themselves. What is needed is for Jesus to be revealed in us by the Father in person. As long as this Event has not taken place within us, our faith risks degenerating into a stubborn ideology or an exacerbated moral rigorism. It remains hesitant, quickly threatened, necessarily mixed with doubt. But one day our hour will come, as it came to Peter. It will be brief, it will be dazzling, and its burning will forever leave traces in our heart. Once we have seen, we will never forget. And we will finally understand why only the Father himself can reveal the Son, and not to the wise and the learned, but only to the little ones (Matt 11:25).

# Twenty-second Sunday of Ordinary Time

## Matthew 16:21-27

*Peter said to Jesus, "You are the Messiah, the Son of the Living God." From that moment on, Jesus began to show his disciples that it was necessary for him to go up to Jerusalem, to suffer greatly at the hands of the elders, the chief priests, and the scribes, and to be killed, and on the third day to be raised. Then Peter took him aside and began to rebuke him, saying, "God forbid, Lord! No such thing will ever happen to you." But he turned and said to Peter, "Get behind me, Satan, for you are an obstacle to me! Your thoughts are not those of God, but of human beings."*

*Then Jesus said to his disciples, "If anyone wishes to come after me, let him deny himself, take up his cross, and follow me. For whoever wishes to save his life will lose it, but whoever loses his life for my sake will save it. What profit is there for one to gain the whole world but lose or forfeit one's life? Or what can one give in exchange for one's life? For the Son of Man will come with his angels in his Father's glory and will repay everyone according to his works."*

Jesus' disciples are headed for a cruel disappointment whose importance they are absolutely unable to divine. It will catch them completely unawares, and Jesus will be at once its cause and its object.

It's only been a few months since they met him for the first time, and this encounter caused their hearts to capsize. They left everything to follow him, sensing an important role for this young, talented rabbi who attracted such great crowds to himself. And, at first, their hopes were not disappointed but rather brilliantly confirmed. The crowds press in on Jesus. He performs healings and miracles so varied and numerous that one cannot remember hearing of any past prophet doing the like. The future is promising and seems assured. On occasion, the disciples even surprise themselves by the quarrels erupting among them as they jealously seek after the most honored places in the future kingdom that Jesus will doubtless establish without further delay.

But wait! Suddenly things seem to have changed. Jesus' success has provoked a muted opposition on the part of the dominant class. People leave him discreetly, they spy on him, they shout at him in public. But above all, and much more worrisome, it is Jesus himself who seems to have changed, at least in the tone and the content of his discourse, as we have just heard in today's Gospel. No longer is it so much a question of the kingdom that has drawn near in Jesus, but of Jesus himself—now promised to sufferings, to execution, and to a mysterious resurrection.

As the apostles still do not understand anything of this resurrection of which Jesus speaks, it is on his suffering and death that they fixate and that they stumble. As usual in such a case, Peter feels authorized to raise a vehement protestation. Not in public, but privately, confidentially. No doubt he imagines that Jesus is passing through a moment of discouragement, that he is in need of comforting words from a friend, words more likely whispered into Jesus' ear than pronounced out loud. But look—Jesus' reaction is just as vehement as Peter's protest: it is even brutal. He turns to look Peter square in the face: "Get behind me, Satan! You are an obstacle to me. Your way of looking at things is that of human beings, not that of God!" Poor Peter! Last Sunday, Jesus congratulated him because God had revealed to him what flesh and blood could never have made him understand. Today, Peter finds himself as destitute as any one of us. It happens still that people accept Jesus as the Messiah. But for Jesus to be truly the Messiah, he must come to such a wretched end—this is what they find particularly unacceptable.

That is not all. Jesus seems to want to make use of Peter's scandalized response as an opportunity to risk a still more disconcerting pronouncement. He will not bear the cross alone. Henceforth, to carry one's own cross in the following of Jesus will be the absolute condition of becoming his disciple. The apostles' disappointment must have been full to the brim, at least if at that time they were already able to understand these words in all their profundity.

The explications that Jesus adds are addressed both to them and to us who, one day or another, will find ourselves inevitably confronted with the same disappointment, ambushed by the same incomprehension, and tempted, like Peter, to take up a private conversation with Jesus, to remonstrate with him against his will, it becoming a stumbling stone that stops us dead on his path. And for good reason: to renounce oneself, to lose one's life, is much more than to be stripped of one's goods; it is to be stripped of oneself, apparently to lose oneself entirely.

Peter could not understand it, still swimming as he was in the euphoria of success. And we, how could we understand it if we were not seared day after day with the image of the crucified, and if we had not already begun to savor, through our own crosses, a foretaste of the life that Jesus promises in exchange for death?

# Twenty-third Sunday of Ordinary Time

## Matthew 18:15-20

*Jesus said to his disciples, "If your brother sins against you, take him aside and point out to him his fault. If he listens to you, you have won over your brother. If he does not listen to you, take with you one or two others so that 'every fact may be established on the testimony of two or three witnesses.' If he does not listen to them, tell the church. If he refuses to listen even to the church, then treat him as you would a Gentile or a tax collector. Amen, I say to you: whatever you bind on earth shall be bound in heaven, and whatever you loose on earth shall be loosed in heaven.*

*"Again, I say to you: if two of you agree on earth about anything for which you are to pray, it will be granted you by my heavenly Father. For whenever two or three are gathered in my name, there am I in the midst of them."*

When two or three believers are gathered in the name of Jesus, everything changes, everything is tipped over. Since Jesus is in the midst of them, their assembly is no longer merely a human assembly; it is the assembly of God, it is the church. The span of the reunion changes as well. It is multiplied exponentially; it expands by the hundreds.

Within such a group, unheard of powers burst forth: "In my name," Jesus promised, "you will cast out demons, you will heal the sick."

Powers not only over human beings, but also, yet more mysteriously, a power over God himself, as announced by today's Gospel: "Everything that you ask in my name, you will receive it from my Father in heaven." The presence of Jesus in our midst, and within his church, confers every day unhoped for, awesome powers that manifest his presence and are already secretly building up the kingdom of his love.

The beginning of today's Gospel alludes to a particular power that Jesus has left in deposit to his church, a power that is, in the most explosive way, the sign of his love: the power of reconciliation and of forgiveness. A summit of love and a summit in Jesus' life. Did he not come among us, did he not die and rise, precisely to fulfill and to announce mercy and forgiveness?

Reading this Gospel attentively, one notices that in its celebration this pardon encompasses, so to speak, three degrees. At the third degree, when a still recalcitrant brother is summoned before the authority of the church, it seems to correspond to the power to bind and to loose that we recognize in the sacrament of reconciliation. But, also according to the Gospel, it is not necessary every time to come to such a pass and have recourse to church authority. In many cases, a word of fraternal correction, of one brother to another or before two or three witnesses, will suffice.

This is one of the most extraordinary divine powers left in trust to every Christian community, when Jesus is present there: the strength of love irresistibly reconciles, reunites, unifies, makes one.

Let us understand this well: not every believer has received power to sacramentally absolve a brother or sister. This is the role of the priest alone. By contrast, every Christian, in the strength of Jesus' name, and by the power of the Holy Spirit, has received a gift that is perhaps no less marvelous and is, in any case, more urgent and more immediately useful: that of being before every one of his brothers and sisters an evident sign of God's forgiveness and tender mercy, and that perhaps long before the need of sacramental confession imposes itself.

It is indeed by this sign of mutual forgiveness that one may recognize the truly evangelical community in whose midst Jesus never ceases to abide. These are communities abounding with good Samaritans and good shepherds—and all the baptized are called to be such—who locate those who have been wounded on the wide path and do not abandon the sheep gone astray, but rather carry them on their own shoulders; whose speech, even in correction, never wounds, never humiliates, never condemns, never discourages, but rather encourages, builds up, edifies, and casts errors and sins unceasingly into the flames of divine mercy. There is no greater joy for God than in this sinner who repents (Luke 15:7) because of the brothers or sisters who, like God himself, know how to forgive relentlessly, not once, not seven times, but seven times seventy times (Matt 18:22). The strength of God's love in a human heart; the strength of God's love in the heart of his church.

# Twenty-fourth Sunday of Ordinary Time

## Matthew 18:21-35

*Peter approached Jesus and asked him, "Lord, if my brother sins against me, how many times must I forgive him? As many as seven times?" Jesus said to him in reply, "I tell you, not seven times, but seven times seventy times.*

*"For the kingdom of God may be likened to a king who wanted to settle accounts with his servants. He began by summoning someone who owed him ten thousand talents (that is, sixty million silver pieces). As the man had no means of repaying him, his master ordered him to be sold, along with his wife, his children, and all his goods, in payment of the debt. Then that servant, falling to his knees, begged his master, saying, 'Be patient with me, and I will pay you back in full.' Moved to compassion, the servant's master let him go and forgave him the debt. But on going out, the servant found one of his fellow servants who owed him one hundred silver pieces. He began to choke him, saying, 'Pay back what you owe!' Falling to his knees, his companion begged him, saying, 'Be patient with me, and I will pay you back.' But the other one refused and had him put into prison until he should reimburse him. When their fellow servants saw this, they were deeply distressed and reported the whole affair to their master. Thereupon, he*

*summoned the servant whose debt he had forgiven and said, 'You wicked servant! I forgave you your entire debt because you begged me to. Should you not then have had mercy on your fellow servant as I had mercy on you?' Then the master, in his anger, ordered the servant to be handed over to the torturers until he should pay off the entire debt.*

*"So will my heavenly Father do to you, unless each of you forgive your brother from your whole heart."*

There are two ways to read this parable of Jesus about forgiving from our whole heart so that, one day, the Father may likewise forgive us. It could be conceived of as a business transaction between us and God: making an effort to forgive others, we can be assured of God's forgiveness in turn. We would thus be in some sense able to impose an obligation upon God, to make him our debtor. Henceforth, we would have a right to his forgiveness. It is likely that in Jesus' day a number of Jews understood the parable in this manner and that, moreover, some Christians still do so today. They forgive in order to receive God's corresponding forgiveness. Jesus accepts this, provisionally. But he is waiting for them at the bend in the road.

This bend is never far away. Of course, in everyday life, it is often easy enough to give pardon. The word itself—*pardon*—has even become [in French] a simple formula of politeness that no longer has anything to do with Jesus' message. Sooner or later, however, more taxing events await us: frustrations whose wounds will require a whole lifetime to develop their scar tissue; nasty tricks that others play on us, injustices that are, literally, "worthy of hanging" [Fr. *pendable*]; crying, truly unforgiveable. Do we only have the right to forgive, perhaps thus making ourselves complicit in the injustice or wronging ourselves? Even though the lips may utter forgiveness, the heart may swell with hatred, more or less appropriately suppressed, that will nonetheless continue to develop in secret, until it risks one day exploding. Psychology even claims that fearful risks are run by thus holding in such a perfectly healthy aggressivity, and that one may pay the price of permanent damage to the personality. Sooner or later, the moment will arrive for us when forgiveness proves impracticable.

How, then, are we to understand Jesus' commandment? Today's parable gives us the key. If the unforgiving servant is condemned, it is not because he refuses to forgive. Jesus knows well that certain kinds of forgiveness are impossible and perhaps even unhealthy. Rather, the servant is condemned because he refuses to forgive even after he had first been forgiven. It is necessary first to have received Jesus' forgiveness if one is to be in a condition to forgive in turn, without doing harm to oneself, and just as Jesus forgives.

Yet to receive Jesus' forgiveness, it is essential first of all to recognize one's own need to be forgiven, to place oneself among the publicans and prostitutes, among the sinners for whose sake alone Jesus came, not to judge them, but to save them (Matt 18:11). It is to know ourselves loved just as we are, without possessing any right to this love. It means feeling just how much his love forestalls us, envelops us, overflows us, and transforms us, far beyond anything we would have dared to ask or hope for. It is to understand that the love of Jesus is so blind that he no longer sees our sins!

Those who would reduce this parable of Jesus to a business transaction—"I will forgive so as to one day receive forgiveness in turn"—are undoubtedly off track. They are headed down a path on which, despite their apparent generosity, they obstruct ever more completely the one path that could have led them to open the door of their heart—the humble path, the narrow (Matt 7:13) and very low gate—of the recognition of their own weakness, the one place where

Jesus has so long awaited them, so that he might grant them a taste of his superabounding love, not only in spite of their sin, but precisely because they are sinners.

This is the one and only way towards the heart: humility. This is the first, inevitable degree of the experience of Christian contemplation. No devotional exercises, no ascetical rigor, no techniques of meditation, whether Eastern or Western, can replace it. The humility of the sinner alone holds the key to contemplative interiority, as also to fraternal forgiveness. For only the love of Jesus, experienced to such a degree, can dissolve the accumulated mountains of hatred in our hearts without doing us any further harm—quite the contrary. For only those who have thus been healed by Jesus' love are able to heal others in turn, with the same love that no longer even sees offenses.

# Twenty-fifth Sunday of Ordinary Time

## Matthew 20:1-16a

*Jesus told this parable: "The kingdom of heaven is like a landowner who went out early in the morning to hire workers for his vineyard. He made an agreement with them to pay them the usual daily wage and then sent them into his vineyard. Going out again at about nine o'clock, he saw others standing idle in the marketplace, and he said to them, 'You too, go into my vineyard, and I will pay you what is just.' So they went. He went out again about noon, and again at three o'clock, and did the same. Finally, at about five o'clock, he went out again and found others standing there to whom he said, 'Why are you standing here idle all day?' They answered him, 'Because no one has hired us.' He said to them, 'You too, go into my vineyard.'*

*"When it was evening, the landowner said to his foreman, 'Summon the laborers and give them their pay, beginning with the last and ending with the first.' Those who had only worked since five o'clock came forward, and each of them received the usual daily wage. When those who had been hired first came forward, they expected that they would receive more, but they too received the usual daily wage. And, on receiving it, they grumbled against the landowner, saying, 'These last ones worked only one hour, but you have*

*made them the equals of us, who bore the day's burden and the heat!' But the master said to one of them, 'My friend, I am not cheating you. Did you not make an agreement with me for the usual daily wage? Take what is yours and go. What if I want to give this one the same as you? Or am I not free to do as I wish with my own money? Is your eye evil because I am good?'*

*"Thus, the last will be first, and the first will be last."*

Could God be unjust? Are not all humans equal before our heavenly Father? Will we not be repaid according to our works and the sufferings we have endured? Does God bestow privileges, give away free passes?

God often disconcerts us. His justice differs from ours, even if the latter has its own legitimacy. It is so different that it sometimes scandalizes us just as the vineyard owner scandalized his laborers in the parable that we have just heard.

However, according to a standard of strict justice, there was really no foundation for scandal. The work contract had been scrupulously respected, and the usual daily wage was an honorable payment in exchange for a full day's work.

The workers' murmuring was based on something else. There had been some who had been there from the early morning and who had, in keeping with their boast, "borne the day's burden and the heat." Then those of the last hour, perhaps numbered among the unemployed and counted as nothing, or lazybones who preferred to dawdle a while before finishing what the first had courageously begun. If the latecomers received the usual daily wage for so little effort, the others could legitimately hope to receive a greater reward. But it was not to be. How can we not be surprised or even protest along with them?

Two possible responses can be offered to their surprise. The first is given by Jesus himself: "Is your eye evil because I am good?" God's justice cannot rest content with the terms defined by a contract. It is kindness, generosity, an excess of mercy. The measure of his gifts, as he himself says, is always "a good measure, firmly packed, pressed down and overflowing" (Luke 6:38). Besides, it is addressed by preference to those who have merited it less than others, who have hardly made the efforts to which most people devote themselves, but for whom a single cry of trusting confidence will suffice, a single look bathed in tears of love. We recognize them: the tax collectors and the prostitutes who will precede us into the kingdom (Matt 21:31). They are named Mary Magdalene, Zachaeus, Matthew, and so many others, including that first of saints, canonized by Jesus himself on the cross, that true laborer of the last hour: the good thief, whom Jesus dispatched to Paradise at that very hour to welcome all those whom his death and resurrection were going to deliver (Luke 23:43).

The second response to this surprise is hidden within our own heart. It depends on where we locate ourselves in this parable. Indeed, as long as we consider ourselves "laborers of the first hour," claiming the right to compensation for services rendered, we cannot help but be shocked by such blatant injustice on God's part, by a master who shows such partiality. But, at the same time, this would be the sign that our heart remains, for the moment, hardened and still knows little of the surprising gentleness of Jesus' love and forgiveness.

The day will come when our heart of stone will be broken at the onset of an ordeal: a failure, for example, perhaps a sin, or simply the humiliating awareness of our radical incapacity to meet the God whom we claim to love. This will be a moment of grace when we finally allow ourselves humbly to be ranged with the laborers of the final hour, following the useless servants, alongside the sinners and the good thief, and even behind them, conscious of having done so little, or even nothing at all, but consenting to be there on that basis, having no right to any payment but only to mercy, to the overwhelming beneficence of God. That is our rightful place.

It will be our joy besides, our greatest and eternal joy. As well as the greatest possible joy for God himself. "For there will be more joy in heaven," Jesus says, "over one sinner who repents than over ninety-nine righteous ones who have no need of repentance" (Luke 15:7).

# Twenty-sixth Sunday of Ordinary Time

## Matthew 21:28-32

*Jesus said to the chief priests and the elders, "What is your opinion? A man had two sons. He went to the first and said to him, 'My child, go and work in the vineyard today.' He responded, 'I will not go.' But afterward, he changed his mind and went. Approaching the second, the father said the same thing. The son replied, 'Yes, sir!' But he did not go. Which of the two did his father's will?" They answered, "The first." Jesus said to them, "Amen, I say to you: tax collectors and prostitutes are entering the kingdom of God before you. For John the Baptist came to you in the way of righteousness, and you did not believe him, but tax collectors and prostitutes did. Yet even when you saw that, you did not then change your mind and repent."*

These two sons in the parable represent two types of human being that we easily identify, two different destinies before God, as well.

The first son would not dare to refuse his father anything. He easily says "yes." A quiet person, accommodating, confident of being his father's favorite. As for deeds that would correspond to this status, he will take his time, drag his feet, postpone. With time, perhaps the command will have been forgotten. He will always keep up appearances.

The other son is much less pleasant to his father. He is headstrong and impulsive. He dares to contradict his father to his face, to violate a direct order. There is nothing servile about him. Before yielding to his father, he feels the overpowering, essential need to confront him, to measure up to him. In the eyes of others, he is the bad son, the nasty boy, he who begins by grumbling and always finds a pretext for backtalk.

But who is he in the eyes of his father? How does his father experience him as he issues his refusal and, above all, how does he take it at the moment when the son throws a "no" back into his face? Curiously, the Gospel says nothing about it. Did the father fall into a violent rage? Did he hint at a violent act? Did he withdraw into a sullen silence? Or did he, on the contrary, dissolve in tears of sorrow, increasing his insistence? All these are attitudes among which, in the father's place, we would have a hard time choosing.

The Gospel tells us nothing about it, except that we can divine something from the unexpected issue that soon follows. The father's reaction—and, in the parable, he stands in for God—must have been such that the son found himself completely disarmed. There had been resistance, a sudden groundless contentiousness. And now, his refusal has melted away like snow in the sunlight before the marvelous warmth that the father spreads abroad, before a tenderness all the more unheard of and efficacious as it seems to have been not only released, but even redoubled, taken to the extreme, by the son's refusal. It is in the face of this very refusal that God's tenderness bursts forth. O marvelous rebellion! O happy fault! O unparalleled grace that the other son, well-behaved and well-scrubbed, cannot know, though he knows very well how to comport himself so as always to seem to say "yes"!

These two sons of the parable are present within each of us: the good-natured one and the nasty one, the righteous and the publican, and we oscillate ceaselessly between the one and the other, desiring so much to keep to the side of the just but blushing in advance, even to the point of becoming vexed sometimes, at repeatedly finding ourselves among the publicans.

Jesus is nevertheless perfectly clear in the foregoing: despite appearances, the righteous one can get off to a bad start. It is the publican who has the better fortune. Along with the prostitutes, he is the one who will precede even Jesus' apostles into the kingdom of God (Matt 21:31).

Not that the publican's path is good. On the contrary, he should sooner or later abandon this way of rebellion. He will change his mind, says the Gospel, but now we can guess how and when: at the moment when he finds himself enveloped, invaded, inundated by the gentle warmth of the paternal tenderness that alone suffices—without ever forcing or breaking anything—to wear down all our resistance.

There is never any cause for us to become discouraged at carrying around the tax collector within us. On the contrary, he is there precisely to be saved and so that, thanks to him, we too can be saved. For it is he alone within us who will one day be able to be encountered by Jesus and receive his forgiveness: "I did not come for the righteous," says Jesus, "but for sinners" (Luke 5:32).

# Twenty-seventh Sunday of Ordinary Time

## Matthew 21:33-43

*Jesus said to the chief priests and the Pharisees, "Hear this parable: there was a certain landowner who planted a vineyard, planted a hedge around it, dug a winepress, and built a watch tower. Then he leased it to tenant farmers and went on a journey. When vintage time had come, he sent his servants to the tenants to obtain the produce of the vineyard. But the tenants seized the servants, beat one of them, killed another, and stoned a third. Again, the vineyard owner sent other servants more numerous than the first, but they treated them in the same way. Finally, he sent them his son, saying to himself, 'They will respect my son.' But on seeing the son, the tenants said to one another, 'This is the heir. Come! Let us kill him, and the inheritance will be ours!' So they seized him, threw him out of the vineyard, and killed him. What, then, will the master of the vineyard do to those tenants when he arrives?" They answered, "He will put those wretched men to a wretched death and lease the vineyard to other tenants who will give him its produce at the proper time." Jesus said to them, "Have you never read this Scripture? 'The stone that the builders rejected has become the cornerstone. By the Lord has this been done, and it is marvelous in our eyes.' Therefore, I tell you, the*

***kingdom of God will be taken from you and given to a people who will produce its fruit."***

The story of God and humanity is a love story, but a love story equally as tormented as that of the vineyard owner and his vine. The vineyard owner loved his vine. He cared for it. He endowed it with all that was necessary to render it productive. He had confided it to the best workers. Alas! It produced only wild grapes. At vintage time, his servants are beaten to death, stoned on two occasions. Then he risks everything in the hope of gaining everything. "They will respect my son," says the vineyard owner to himself, who resolves to send them what is most dear to himself. After failure upon failure, it seems to him the only remaining solution. But he is struck by yet another blow, the worst of all: his own son, he too, is put to death, while these tenants hope to seize the inheritance.

Up to this point, the chief priests and the Pharisees ought to have been able to grasp the meaning of Jesus' parable. It was transparent. The prophets had compared Israel to a vine and God to a winemaker. Throughout history, God's patience with his vineyard had been unlimited because his love had been unlimited. But in a thousand different ways, Israel had turned a deaf ear to its God. His most marvelous gifts? Israel had misused them. God's wonderful plan for Israel? The latter had made of it an obstacle. Like the winemaker of the parable with his vine, God had experienced nothing but rebuffs and failures on the part of his chosen people. But just as unceasingly, God had continued to take up the torn thread of Sacred History, to weave its fabric, believing in the potential masterpiece. However great Israel's disaffection, God had never abandoned it. As the psalmist sings, "They were not faithful to his covenant, but he, being merciful, forgave them instead of destroying them" (Ps 77:38). Every failure is merely a passing peripeteia for God. Indeed, it forms part of Sacred History, for nothing but human failure can cast God's astonishing love into such sharp relief.

Even when human beings dare to attack God's own Son: this is what the parable insinuates at the end but that Jesus' audience, for the moment, cannot yet understand. Later, they will understand to what extent the drama between God and humanity, between the winemaker and his vine, is bound up with his own Son, Jesus. "They will respect my son," God had thought in the lovely candor of his paternal love. For he, as Saint Paul would one day say, "had loved the world so much that he did not spare his own Son but gave him up for us all." But to no avail. The Son came to his own, but his own recognized neither him nor the Father's love that was manifested in him. They put him to death just as they had done to the Father's other emissaries before him. And once again, for the very last time, the excessive love met defeat at the hand of human refusal.

At least, apparent defeat. For between God and humanity, defeat only serves to enable the greater triumph of love, the Father's love for the Son, the Son's love for the Father, the love of both the Father and the Son for us all. "Have you never read the Scriptures?" Jesus explains to them, " 'The stone that the builders rejected has become the cornerstone? By the Lord has this been done, and it is marvelous in our eyes.' "

Yes, this history of love, of the relations between God and each one of us, is always a more or less tormented history, a history punctuated by numerous defeats that God absorbs from us. But a history that, amazingly, from one seeming fiasco to the next, rebounds relentlessly, the wonders of God's love being never exhausted. It is he who transforms weakness into strength, sin into thanksgiving, and defeat into the victory of love. Truly, it is here, every day: the Lord's own work, marvelous in our eyes.

# Twenty-eighth Sunday of Ordinary Time

## Matthew 22:1-14

*Jesus told these parables: "The kingdom of heaven is like a king who held a wedding banquet for his son. He sent his servants to invite the guests, but the latter did not want to come. Again, he sent other servants, saying to those invited, 'Behold, the banquet is prepared: my bulls and fattened calves have been killed, and everything is ready. Come to the feast!' But they disregarded the message and went away, one to his farm, another to his business. The others laid hold of the servants, mistreated them, and killed them. The king flew into a rage. He sent his troops, put those murderers to death, and burned their city. Then he said to his servants, 'The wedding feast is ready, but those invited were not worthy. Go, therefore, into the streets and alleyways and invite to the wedding feast everyone whom you meet, bad and good alike, that my hall may be filled with guests.'*

*"When the king entered to greet his guests, he saw a man not dressed in a wedding garment, and he said to him, 'My friend, how is it that you came in without a wedding garment?' But he was reduced to silence. Then the king said to his servants, 'Bind his hands and feet and cast him into the darkness outside, where there will be wailing and grinding of teeth.'*

*"For many are called, but few are chosen."*

In this parable, there were those who were invited and those who were not. Those invited had a right to be there: a people chosen by God, bearers of the promise, children of the covenant, firstborn heirs, a noble olive tree of its own stock and producing choice fruits.

And then there are the others, those who can claim no such right, who could have supposed themselves to count for nothing with God, wild and inferior olive trees.

When the wedding feast of God and his people drew near, the chosen ones held their invitation cheap. They were busy, distracted, burdened with affairs. God's pressing and repeated invitations only served to irritate them, even to render them aggressive. They rejected the messengers and went so far as to murder his own son. Had a passionate love ever been so cruelly mocked?

But God's love is inexhaustible! It is never cut short by any evil; nor is it ever lacking in ruses by means of which to triumph. Henceforth it is to the formerly uninvited, to those without any claim, that God addresses himself: to the man or woman in the street, to whoever presents themselves at the crossroads. None of them really deserved it. They must have been surprised to find themselves assembled in the festal hall, so surprised that one of them had not even thought to vest himself in a wedding garment.

We too ought to be equally surprised to find ourselves gathered for the wedding banquet. We did not form part of the people of God, chosen from centuries past. We too were not merely "the man in the street" but complete strangers to the promise, not having deserved at all to be there, wild olive branches grafted onto the noble trunk, perpetual immigrants in our new homeland.

Such has been God's mercy, as Saint Paul explains to us in the Letter to the Galatians. Did those who were first called fall away? It was so that, one day, God might again show them mercy. If God has called us in their stead, it is so that his mercy might shine out in us Gentiles more wonderfully still. "For," writes Paul, "God has constrained all in sin, that he might have mercy on all" (Gal 3:22).

Yet we are bound by one condition: that of wearing a wedding garment. No one can participate in the meal without taking the trouble to dress for it. This garment is, simply, Jesus himself, and there could never be another. "Strip off the old man," again says Saint Paul, "and clothe yourselves with the new man, created in Jesus Christ" (Eph 4:24). Did we have no right to the wedding feast? He, in person, is the guarantee of our right. Did we not have the promises granted to the people of the Old Covenant? It is he who is their fulfillment. Were we lacking in all merit? He is the wedding garment who covers our nakedness with the merits of his glory.

Not only did we lack merits before we were called, but, even since our call, we have not ceased to imitate the negligence of those previously called. Truly, we have not been better than the Jews! We too are quite often distracted, bogged down, unavailable. We live on the exterior of ourselves, we easily turn our back on the feast that has been prepared, on the nuptial chamber whose entrance lies in the depths of our hearts, there where the Bridegroom awaits us at every moment, Jesus; there, where we are temples of the Spirit (1 Cor 3:16), who is the one bond of love who attaches us to Jesus and who, in Jesus, unites us to the Father and to all human beings. This is the one thing necessary, and it suffices (Luke 10:42). Our charism is to be content with this. All the rest is excess (Matt 6:33).

Fortunately, God has not exhausted his store of loving stratagems for us either. Every day, he presses his invitation, more tenderly, more irresistibly: "The table has been prepared. Come to the wedding feast!"

# Twenty-ninth Sunday of Ordinary Time

## Matthew 22:15-21

*The Pharisees took counsel against Jesus to try to trap him in speech. They sent their disciples to him, accompanied by the Herodians. "Master," they said, "we know that you are a truthful man and that you teach God's way in accordance with the truth, and you show no partiality, for you are no respecter of persons. Tell us your opinion, then: is it permitted to pay taxes to Caesar or not?" But Jesus, knowing their malice, said in reply, "Why are you testing me, you hypocrites? Show me the coin that pays the temple tax." And they produced the coin for him. He said to them. "Whose image is this, and whose inscription?" They answered: "Caesar's." Then he said to them, "Then render to Caesar what belongs to Caesar, and to God what belongs to God."*

The one who mints a coin inscribes his name upon it and engraves his image. Money is always made in the image of someone who has power over it.

If money bears Caesar's image, then it belongs to Caesar, it is his due. Caesar has the right to levy a tax, and Jesus will not refuse to pay it: render to Caesar what belongs to Caesar. Even if Caesar is the enemy, the money that he causes to flow freely in the occupied territories belongs to him. Whoever would make use of it therefore owes Caesar his due, even if the latter is the occupier.

This response is so obvious that, in Jesus' eyes, it seems not to respond to the real question, for another question is concealed behind the one that is posed to him. One cannot serve two masters: God and money. Also, the real question for Jesus, the only one that matters to him, is not what one ought to pay to Caesar, but what one ought to pay to God. One renders to Caesar that which bears his image; one renders to God what is made in the image of God.

But his adversaries have not taken account of the fact that it is he, Jesus, before and more than anyone else, who is the very image of God: this Jesus whom they are trying to put in an awkward position. They have not perceived God's stamp on his humanity. For Jesus has not merely been fashioned to the image and likeness of God, as were the first man Adam and his descendants (Gen 1:26), but he is himself this image in its fullness, the substantial image (Col 1:15). In his human body, in his face that must have had an unforgettable beauty and nobility, Jesus is the refulgence of the glory of God. In him the fullness of divinity dwells corporeally (Col 2:9). From now on, it suffices to cast one's gaze on Jesus to plunge into the depths of God: "Philip, whoever has seen me has seen the Father" (John 14:9). In Jesus, God has placed himself within our reach and offered himself to us.

He is the Lord, and there is no other. Caesar offers him no competition. Three times in our first reading God made the same declaration through the mouth of the prophet Isaiah: "There is no God but me. From East to West, let everyone know: I am the Lord, and there is no other."

Caesar cannot substitute himself for Jesus, nor can money and wealth, those idols renounced by the believer. The believer's confidence is never placed in Caesar or in the money made in his image. The believer knows in whom he has placed his trust and to whom he has delivered himself: to Jesus, the precious metal of humanity impressed with God's effigy, to Jesus, who loved him and gave himself for him (Gal 2:20).

Every believer will one day have to make a choice between Caesar and Jesus. Sometimes the choice is obvious; more often, it is subtle and obscure. But no Christian can avoid it entirely. For between these two, God and money, one cannot love one without hating the other, and it is Jesus himself who has affirmed this (Luke 16:13). And this is all the more true inasmuch as the one who chooses between them thus opts for or against herself. For she too has been stamped with an image, not that of Caesar, but that of God, just like Jesus. If she opts for the image of Caesar, she will end up resembling Caesar, and the image of God in her will deteriorate little by little. If she opts for Jesus, she will be progressively renewed in his image and be completely conformed to him (2 Cor 3:18). The radiance of God's glory will henceforth appear on her face. Belonging to God, she will be entirely rendered to God.

# Thirtieth Sunday of Ordinary Time

## Matthew 22:34-40

*When the Pharisees saw how Jesus had silenced the Sadducees, they gathered together, and one of them, a scholar of the law, posed this question to him: "Teacher, what is the greatest commandment in the law?" Jesus said to him in reply, "You shall love the Lord your God with all your heart, with all your soul, and with all your mind. This is the first and greatest commandment. The second is like it: You shall love your neighbor as yourself. The whole law and the prophets depend on these two commandments."*

It's a Pharisee who poses the question to Jesus. They have just learned how, by means of one of his responses, he has silenced the Sadducees, their rivals. A good opportunity: they hope now to draw Jesus into their party, for the question expresses perfectly their major preoccupation: observing the commandments. Hence the importance, in their eyes, of knowing the greatest of the commandments. Whoever succeeds in observing it perfectly will be, they suppose, greatest in the eyes of God.

Jesus does not put them in the wrong. There is indeed, he concedes, a greatest among the commandments: "You shall love the Lord, your God, with all your heart," a textual citation of the Pentateuch. There are even two of them, and they are like one another: "You shall love your neighbor as yourself." Jesus goes farther still. Basically, he adds, there are no other commandments than these, for together they express the entirety of the law and the prophets: "The whole law and the prophets depend on these two commandments."

A greatest commandment? Yes, even two of them. But curiously, they are now no more than invitations to love, commandments transformed into love. The Gospel does not say whether the Pharisee was satisfied with Jesus' answer or whether, perhaps, he felt himself trapped in his turn, he who had wanted to set a trap for Jesus. He would have more easily understood, surely, that one must more scrupulously maintain this observance, respect that rite, refrain from such and such an evil deed. But what can one do to have sentiments of love for God and for one's neighbor? Don't we say that love cannot be commanded, that we either love someone or we don't, and that to love others out of duty is the worst thing we can inflict on them and is, besides, unconvincing and unrequited? The love commandment is an impossible commandment, in the eyes of the good Pharisee, a perfection beyond his reach. How much simpler it would be, more reassuring, just to have some things to do and others to avoid.

By summing up the whole law in the law of love, Jesus has totally shaken the moral code—seemingly rigorous, but in fact easy and basically superficial—of the Pharisee. Jesus' commandments appear to him as of another order entirely, and their observance will entirely elude the person whose heart of stone has not yet been transformed into a heart of flesh and who has not yet been indwelt by the tenderness of the Holy Spirit.

If only there were only the first commandment and not also the second that is like it! With the help of a certain interior discipline, one might endeavor to concentrate oneself on a certain idea of God, to extract from the heart some feelings of reverence, of fear, of admiration, even a hint of love, with respect to God Most High, the Almighty, who creates and rules the universe. All that, of which the Pharisee would perhaps be capable, would still be far removed from the love that Jesus suggests to him in his response. The proof of this lies in the second commandment. To love, to the fullest extent, a distant God—but how to love, in all truth, the neighbor at our elbow, always a bit irritating, a rival, an intriguer, faithless, sometimes treacherous? How to love such neighbors, not in words or with the mouth alone, but from the heart and in deeds? The Pharisee is right: such a morality surpasses every possible morality. It is of another order. It is an entirely new commandment that supposes a radically recreated heart, transformed by God's tenderness, that is, by the Holy Spirit in person, a heart in which "that love of God has been poured out by the Holy Spirit who has been given to us" (Rom 5:5).

And the perfection that Jesus announces is hence not that of the Pharisees, it is that of God: "Be perfect just as your Father in heaven is perfect" (Matt 5:48). It is also expressed as "Be merciful," that is, be overflowing with tenderness just as your heavenly Father abounds with tenderness (Luke 6:36).

# Thirty-first Sunday of Ordinary Time

## Matthew 23:1-12

*Jesus said to the crowd and to his disciples, "The scribes and the Pharisees have taken their seat on the chair of Moses. Do, therefore, and observe whatever they tell you. But do not follow their example, for they preach but they do not practice. They tie up heavy burdens hard to carry and lay them on people's shoulders, but they themselves will not lift a finger to move them. They perform all their works to be seen by others: they widen their phylacteries and lengthen their tassels; they love places of honor at banquets, seats of honor in synagogues, and the salutation 'Rabbi.' As for you, do not be called Rabbi, for you have but one teacher and you are all brothers. Call no one on earth your father, for you have but one Father in heaven. Do not be called 'Master,' for you have but one master, the Christ. The greatest among you will be your servant. For whoever exalts himself will be humbled, but whoever humbles himself will be exalted."*

This Gospel brings home to us just how much Jesus has changed the face of the earth, and not just the earth, but the face of humanity as well, the relations that tie us together, the roles that we play, and even the names that we give to one another.

Some of the most common names: *Master, Father*. We thought we knew what they signified and to whom we could address them in all good faith. Jesus has just taught us that their meaning has changed and that we can no longer use them as before. Understood in the sense in which we knew them, they are no longer any more than the shadow of themselves, or rather the shadow of another, of the one who has just passed among us, who has so to speak voided their previous meaning to fill them with himself; they are the shadow of Jesus, or of his Father who is in heaven.

The Jews might well have been astonished, they who belonged to a thoroughly hierarchical community, with chief priest, priests, doctors of the law. But Jesus seems to be abolishing this hierarchy: one unique Rabbi, only one Master for everyone, himself; one sole Father as well, he who is in heaven; and all distinctions of rank or dignities nullified: "You are all brothers," since I am here, and since my Father too is here.

From now on, the relationship that exists between Jesus and each one of us is so strong that any other relationship that exists can bear fruit only by virtue of this one. Jesus and his Father have interposed themselves between us and others to such an extent that we can no longer truly reach them except by passing through Jesus and his Father, all reduced or promoted to the rank of universal brother or sister.

There is still more. If a hierarchy must still subsist within Jesus' community—and surely it will be necessary—it too will be totally turned upside down in relation to the hierarchical norms of earthly societies and, again, inverted by reason of Jesus and the example that he left us during his earthly sojourn. Of course, he is our Rabbi and our Master. But he was our Master in making himself the "Servant." "You call me Master, and rightly so," Jesus will say to his apostles, and yet, "I am among you as one who serves." Master, yes, but because he is the Servant, the absolute, unequaled servant who so greatly humbled himself at his disciples' feet on the eve of his passion, who chose the last place to that extent, who humbled himself even to the point of accepting death, death on a cross, so that every disciple who commits himself to follow him on the same path of abasement will be able to replicate merely a faint and quite imperfect trace thereof.

Nevertheless, all hierarchy in the Christian community must henceforth pass by this way of abasement, as paradoxical as that may appear. Jesus has just reminded us of this: "The greatest among you will be your servant" (Mark 10:43). An invisible hierarchy, but the only real one, to which corresponds only feebly, by the strength of things and the weakness of human beings, a visible hierarchy of whatever sort. It is the fool in Christ who is henceforth the wise one and who teaches truly. It is the littlest who is the greatest. It is the poorest one who is richest in God's treasures. It is the sinner who precedes those who think themselves righteous. It is the one who prays in hiddenness who secretly animates the progress of the church and even that of the world. It is those who lie prostrate at the feet of their brothers and sisters, who are perhaps rejected by them, who precede them all.

Why? Because, as Père de Foucauld said, "Jesus has claimed for himself the last place, so that no one can take it from him," and because it is only there that we can join him. "Whoever exalts himself will be humbled, but whoever humbles himself" like Jesus "will be exalted" (Luke 18:14).

# Thirty-second Sunday of Ordinary Time

## Matthew 25:1-13

*Jesus spoke to his disciples about his return, telling them this parable: "The kingdom of heaven will be like ten virgins invited to a wedding, who took their lamps and went to meet the bridegroom. Five of them were foolish, and five were wise. The foolish ones took along no oil for their lamps, whereas the wise ones brought oil. As the bridegroom was long delayed, they all grew tired and fell asleep. At about midnight, a cry was heard: 'Behold, the bridegroom! Go out to meet him!' Then all the virgins awoke and trimmed their lamps. The foolish ones implored the wise, 'Give us some of your oil, for our lamps are going out.' But the wise ones replied, 'No, for there is not enough both for us and for you. Go rather to the merchants and buy some for yourselves.' As they were going off to buy it, the bridegroom arrived. Those who were ready entered the banquet hall with him, and then the door was locked. After a while, the other virgins arrived in turn and cried out, 'Lord, Lord, open the door for us!' But he said in reply, 'Amen, I say to you: I do not know you.'*

*"Therefore, stay awake, for you know neither the day nor the hour."*

In creating the world, and humanity at the heart of the world, God invented time. Time does not exist for God but is rather connatural to human beings, who need it in order to be and to reach their potential. . .

And first of all, to be born. Nine months are required for a baby to take shape, peacefully, in the womb of its mother. Some more time elapses before the first smile, and still more before the child takes its first steps and, again, before its first word. Every age will bring its discoveries, but years will pass before the child learns to become independent, to create, to love someone beyond its parents.

Time is especially needed in learning to love. And to deepen a love that has been chosen once and for all, a great deal of time will be necessary, many years, a whole lifetime of waiting and faithfulness. For time has been given to us principally for love. Love between human beings, but also love between human beings and God. Learning to love takes time. With human beings, who are so changeable, and with a God who is so often hidden, entirely beyond our reach, time is almost the only language available by which human beings can give expression to their love. Time is, in effect, called to become a word of love.

The parable in today's Gospel shows us how God plays very delicately, very adroitly, with time. The nuptials at issue are those celebrated between his Son and the church, between Jesus and each believer. Through Jesus, God entered personally into human time, at a precise moment of human history, and this history has been thus permanently marked. Marked all the more because, for the moment, Jesus has only passed through time, for the duration of a human life. He came, but he also departed. Above all, he will return. And the time that must yet flow downstream, before us, is going nowhere else than to the encounter of his return. It has no meaning except in terms of Jesus' return. It is entirely stretched out towards him, and the church too stretches forward in tension. It waits in patience, confident, bewildered, until he comes. And it can do nothing else.

And behold, henceforth time, for each of us, is devoted exclusively to love. A time that keeps watch for love. It was the only activity that the virgins of the parable were waiting for, those invited to the nuptials of Jesus. It was enough for them to wait and to hold themselves in readiness. For the bridegroom tarried, says Jesus. Nothing surprising about that. Here below, Jesus tarries still. For that is the way that God plays with human time, which every love here below needs to prove itself true. A love that is not a thunderclap, a superficial emotion, will produce a slow-burning fire. Only time, and waiting, and patient vigilance will plumb its depths that elude the feelings but emerge one day at the—as yet unsuspected—wedding feast with Jesus, still scarcely divined, who awaits us behind the door.

And if the wait is prolonged, that is certainly a trial, but also an opportunity. For it must separate those who know how to love from those who stumble over love. The virgins did not all respond to the bridegroom's delay in the same way. When the cry rang out, some had recourse to their surplus oil, while the others did not. The former entered into the banquet hall; the others remained outside the door. Jesus does not explain to us the meaning of this oil, but we may surmise that it has to do with love and with waiting. In the course of this prolonged waiting and its attendant boredom, some began to have doubts, and, in the end, Jesus no longer recognizes them. Throughout the same long period of waiting and boredom, the others continued to believe in Jesus' love. Their faith touched his heart. Their belief in love saved them (1 John 4:16).

# Thirty-third Sunday of Ordinary Time

## Matthew 25:14-30

*Jesus was speaking to his disciples about his return, and he told them this parable: "A man went on a journey. Before departing, he summoned his servants and entrusted to them his goods. To one he gave five talents, to another two, and to a third one, to each according to his ability. Then he departed. At once, the servant who had received five talents went off and traded with them to earn five more. Likewise, the one who had received two talents made use of them to earn an additional two. But the one who had received one talent dug a hole in the ground and buried his master's money.*

*"After a long time had passed, the master returned and settled accounts with his servants. The one who had received five talents came forward and said, 'Lord, you gave me five talents: behold, I have earned five more.' His master said in reply, 'Well done, good and faithful servant! Because you have been faithful in little things, I will entrust you with great matters. Enter into the joy of your lord.'*

*"Then the one who had received two talents came forward and said, 'Lord, you gave me two talents: behold, I have earned two more.' His master said in reply, 'Well done, good and faithful servant! Because you have been faithful*

*in little things, I will entrust you with great matters. Enter into the joy of your lord.'*

*"Then the one who had received one talent came forward and said, 'Lord, I knew that you were a hard man: you reap where you did not sow and gather where you did not scatter. Therefore, I was afraid. So I took your money and buried it in the ground. Here it is. You have back what is yours.' Then his master said to him in reply, 'You wicked, lazy servant! So you knew that I reap where I did not sow and gather where I did not scatter? Why, then, did you not put my money in the bank, so that on my return I might receive it back with interest? Therefore, take the talent from him and give it to the one who has ten. For to the one who has, more will be given, and he will abound. But from the one who has not, even what he has will be taken away. And as for this good-for-nothing servant, cast him into the darkness outside, where there will be wailing and grinding of teeth!'"*

It is not by means of our own goods that we may hope to enter Jesus' kingdom. For the goods of the kingdom are incommensurable with anything we ourselves could bring there. That is why, as in the parable that we have just heard, it is God himself who takes the initiative, and the goods that he distributes to us are his own. Indeed, he does much more than merely distribute them to us: as the Gospel has just specified, he entrusts them to us.

The nuance is important. If God entrusts us with his goods, it means that he has chosen to place his confidence in us and that he expects one thing from us: that we in turn place our confidence in him. This is what happened with the first and the second servants in the parable. Jesus congratulates them: "Well done, good and faithful servant! You have trusted me in little things; I will entrust you with greater matters. Enter into my joy."

And precisely this is the amazing thing, the perennial miracle of these goods that God entrusts to us: they multiply of themselves, they grow without our knowing it, they abound sometimes even in spite of us. There is, however, one condition: that through all these goods and graces received, we dare to place our confidence in the one who first places his confidence in us, that is, in God. "You have trusted me in little things," God will say to us, "I will entrust you with greater matters." And what is still more astonishing, "You possess some of my goods, I will add unto you still more," and "to the one who has more will be given, and he will abound." Marvelous largesse and munificence of God, shocking to the norms of human equity, always greater than our desires, disproportionate to the insignificance of our works.

To dare to have confidence in God, through his grace: that this is indeed the message of the parable is confirmed by what happens to the third servant. With him, things turn out differently. And yet, in a sense, the third servant has less to fear than the first two. He had received but a single talent. For one talent, however, he had become accountable. But behold, he does not dare to play the game of confidence that is, at bottom, the game of love. He is distrustful, afraid. The relationship between himself and his master must have gone south at some point. Already he is no longer the trusting servant but has become a slave, terror-stricken in advance, and the idea would not even occur to him that the master, by confiding to him a portion of his property, was at bottom indicating the secret desire to make of him a friend.

Besides, the image of God that he has forged for himself will scarcely allow him such a measure of trust. It is truly horrible. Not only does it show itself unjust towards God, but it emerges as a veritable blasphemy. Nothing could pain God more, or even paralyze him: "You are a hard man," he is thus reproached; "You reap where you did not sow. I was afraid, so I went and buried your talent in the ground." What an admission! The third servant was afraid of God. He did not dare to believe in the grace that had been given him. Whereas this grace bears fruit of itself for the heart that welcomes it with trust, it is rendered sterile, so to speak, for the heart that is seized by fear, that thinks only of the possible chastisement, who cloaks God in the garb of pitiless magistrate. Grace is truly grace because it is without calculation.

Marvelous power of grace, astonishing fecundity of mercy, ready to renew each day its miracles in our hearts—on the sole condition that we dare to consent to it, as we forget our fears and simply give thanks. To dare to consent to love suffices for God to suddenly double down, ten talents for five, four for two, "for he is good, for his love endures forever."

# Sunday of Christ the King

## Matthew 25:31-46

*Jesus was speaking to his disciples of his return: "When the Son of Man comes in his glory, and all the angels with him, he will take his seat on the throne of glory and all the nations will be assembled before him. And he will separate them from each other, as a shepherd separates the sheep from the goats: he will place the sheep on his right and the goats on his left.*

*"Then he will say to those on his right, 'Come, you blessed by my Father, and inherit the kingdom prepared for you from the foundation of the world. For I was hungry and you gave me food, thirsty and you gave me drink, a stranger and you welcomed me, naked and you clothed me, sick and you visited me, in prison and you came to see me!'*

*"Then the righteous will say to him in reply, 'Lord, when did we see you hungry and give you food, or thirsty and give you drink? When did we see you a stranger and welcome you, or naked and clothe you? When did we see you sick or in prison and visit you?'*

*"And the king will say to them in reply, 'Amen, I say to you, as often as you did it for one of the least of my brothers or sisters, you did it for me.'*

*"Then he will say to those on his left, 'Depart, you accursed, into the eternal fire prepared for the devil and his angels. For I was hungry and you gave me no food, thirsty*

*and you gave me no drink, a stranger and you did not welcome me, naked and you did not clothe me, ill or in prison, and you did not visit me.'*

*"Then they will answer and say. 'Lord, when did we see you hungry or thirsty, naked or a stranger, ill or in prison, and not minister to your needs?' And he will reply, 'Amen, I say to you, whenever you failed to do it for the least of my brothers or sisters, you failed to do it for me.'*

*"And these will go off to eternal punishment, but the righteous to eternal life."*

"Jesus seated on the throne of his glory": thus does the Gospel of Matthew describe him at the time of the Last Judgment. Jesus comes, with a choir of angels for his entourage, and takes possession of his royal throne before the assembled nations. The scene is hardly less explicit than its development by Saint Paul that we heard in the second reading. There too, Jesus reigns after his resurrection. He has triumphed over all his enemies, now reduced to being his footstool. There remains for him only to annihilate death and to hand over the kingdom thus renewed to his Father, solemnly submitting himself to him, so that "God may be all in all."

There is no doubt: Jesus is king, and he reigns. In the eyes of the people, however, who find themselves gathered before him, this royalty of Jesus does not lack an element of surprise. Of course, at this final hour, they contemplate it in its self-evident truth. But they learn, at the same time, that this royalty now so resplendent was for a long time kept secret. Jesus was always their king, but a king kept hidden from their eyes as long as he lived upon earth. A king, besides, whom the majority of them, even among the best of them, had been unable to recognize in their time.

Jesus was nevertheless already truly their king, and even a king present at their side whom they could have encountered and honored as often as they wished.

It is true that some of the Jews, during his lifetime, in their euphoria at his early miracles, had wanted to make him king—but a king merely destined to liberate the Jewish nation from the Roman occupier. Jesus had never been caught in this trap, not even in the desert before Satan, who presented this as the subtlest of his temptations. It is true also that this project of political kingship remained attached to his person, since this was the chief accusation that the chief priests charged him with before the Roman procurator, as the latter would be little concerned with the additional charge of blasphemy that the Sanhedrin lodged against him. As a good defender of Caesar's interests, Pilate had been cut to the quick by this accusation, to the point that he found it necessary to focus his interrogation of Jesus on this point—"Are you the king of the Jews?" thus giving Jesus an opportunity at once to solemnly affirm and to deny: yes, he is a king, but his kingship is not of this world and poses no risk to the Roman emperor (John 18:33). Jesus was at the same time giving to the soldiery an opportunity to turn this royal claim into a sad mockery (John 19:3).

Yes, Jesus is king, but a hidden king, as much for the Jews as for the representatives of Rome. It is not until the end of time that his kingship will be perfectly manifested, to the surprise of all those—us included—who rubbed shoulders with him for so long a time without recognizing him. It is Jesus himself who reveals to us where he is found concealed at present, the hidden king of a kingdom that so many earthly hierarchies and grandeurs provisionally shield from our eyes. "The least of my brothers and sisters" (Matt 25:40), the ones behind whom Jesus keeps himself hidden. It is with them that he identifies. The disciples could have remembered this. From time to time, Jesus alluded to it: was not "the least in the kingdom" declared to be greater than John the Baptist, who was greatest among those born of women (Luke 7:28)? Did he not say that the kingdom belonged exclusively to little children and to those who resembled them (Matt 18:3)?

From now on, there is no room for doubt: Jesus is now present among all the "least ones" whom he recognizes as his brothers and sisters. If they suffer hunger or thirst, if they are sick or persecuted and thrown into prison, it is Jesus who unites them to himself and appeals to us in their person (Matt 25:40). Our king is the brother of the lowly, he is close to those who call upon him. More than that: he and they are one. That is why the poor go before us into his kingdom (Matt 21:31), whereas we, the rich, can only follow them in the measure that we have been able to recognize him in them.